The End of November

Growing Up With Domestic Violence

NICOLE A. SHARPE

authorHOUSE®

AuthorHouse™
1663 Liberty Drive
Bloomington, IN 47403
www.authorhouse.com
Phone: 1-800-839-8640

First published by AuthorHouse 5/17/2010

ISBN: 978-1-4520-1151-6 (e)
ISBN: 978-1-4520-1847-8 (sc)

Cover illustration by Louis Ebarb

Printed in the United States of America
Bloomington, Indiana

This book is printed on acid-free paper.

INTRO

Hi. My name is Ward of the Court. At least that's how the State of New York Child Welfare Services identified me from the age of 15. Then, I was literally on my own. But the feeling of being on my own arose from as far back as I could remember. My parents were too caught up in their confusion to realize that an impressionable child was growing underneath their tattered wings. I grew up in a "lower middle-classed" home, according to societal standards. To the outside world, we were a picturesque family. But when the doors or should I say bars, slammed shut, it was like being in prison. I was subjected to my father's constant abuse of my mother; verbal, emotional and physical and she in turn, heaped that frustration upon me. This was especially true when my father purposely treated me with love and attention and contrasted me to her in order to basically piss her off. Because it was a dysfunctional household, we did not play out the regular "family roles". My father was the "ticking time bomb terrorist", my mother was the "crime victim" and my assailant at times and I was the "fly on the wall" that got pulled into the chaos on occasions by both if it benefited them. The worst part about the whole arrangement is that I loved them.

I have been meaning to write about the shattered episodes of my childhood for a while now but I've been putting it off because it is so difficult to revisit. Right now, I can feel my whole body gently shiver beneath my skin. Although it is not easy, I am motivated by all the survivors and victims of domestic abuse including the most silent of victims, the children orphaned by domestic violence. My goal is for them to realize that they are not alone and to help them to see that they can make a life out there for themselves. Beyond the biological parents, beyond the craziness all around them, there is a shaft of light that is beckoning for their happiness. I have not written in the most conventional of orders but as the memories come to me. My name is Nicole Alaina Sharpe and this is my life growing up with Domestic Violence - The End of November.

To Mommy

and all the victims and survivors of

Domestic Abuse including

The Children

A Special Thank You

To Mya Papaya and Tylie Wylie

who show me the meaning of True Love

everyday

THE END OF NOVEMBER
By Nicole A. Sharpe

Cold night, Cold floor, Stiff wind, White lights,
Silence.
My mommy sleeping like a baby in a pool of
blood
Her hair in two corners of the room
And My daddy standing over her

He painted the walls with her generosity,
goodness, joy and peace
The carpet drenched with her laughter

Time continues in slow motion
Enveloped in this superhuman suspense
My mind is spent
And my whole world is bent

His calculating camouflage made him into
An innocent witness to a crime, so sublime
That he fooled himself into thinking he could
fly away
Like a crow in midday
Stealing young corn

But beyond him, I mourn, for my siblings
Who look at the child in me and call her Mama

Yes it was a Cold night, Cold floor, Stiff wind,
White lights,
Silence
It was the End of November.

PART I

Before

Chapter One

FIRST MEMORIES

M Y FIRST MEMORY IS A dream; a dream of me falling down a flight of stairs in slow motion in my parent's first apartment. I was about three years old, still sleeping in a crib. Every time I would have this dream, I would fearfully jump out of my sleep, clasping the ivory bars of my crib to stand up and then jump into my parent's bed which was up against one side of my crib. A wall was on the other side.

In the dream, everything is a dreary, yellow and the air feels like oatmeal; very thick, slowing every tumble down the stairs and just before I reached the bottom, I always woke up. As an adult I tried to assess this dream in a positive manner. The fact that I never hit the bottom, to me meant that in life I will never allow myself to hit rock bottom. Each tumble down the steps surely does hurt, as in life, we always experience painful experiences such as the death of a loved one, never knowing your parents, being a victim of abuse and just feeling alone, but we will never hit the bottom where we can not go on anymore. That is the positive attitude that we have to have toward life.

Chapter Two

THE ALTERNATE UNIVERSE

WE COULDN'T READ THE BIBLE. He wouldn't let us. We weren't allowed to read any kind of fiction because according to my father, "Fictional stories will do nothing to help you in life." Because he saw the Bible as fiction, he forbid us from reading it. He encouraged us to read the dictionary and the large volumes of encyclopedias and science reference books that he ordered for us. These books took up all the room in our bedroom library. I hated reading the dictionary at first, but then, like everything else, I started to get used to it. I found enjoyment in finding out the meanings and origins of new words and I became hooked to reference books as they fulfilled my need to know about the world around me.

5

Back to the Bible- My father told us that if he caught us reading it, he would throw it through the window. He meant this literally. These weren't just words. I believed him completely because one day when he came home from work, he went over to our retro yellow rotary phone in our kitchen, felt that it was warm and estimated in his mind that my mother was on it with a friend for a long period of time. Somehow, he made a correlation: the higher the level of warmth, the longer the duration of a call, thus the greater my mother's interest in the person on the other end. He made it clear on many occasions that he did not want my mother talking to her friends on the phone. Now that I am looking back, I realize that he always had to be the center of attention in our house. This gave him power; power that he felt he didn't have in the real world. So, he created an alternate world in our home where he was the Hitler, the Gaddafi, the Saddam; figures that he admired and talked about in a glorified manner by the way.

Anyway, he proceeded to rip the old yellow rotary phone out of the wall and throw it on the front lawn for all to see. His rage must have made him blind and act on impulse because he certainly did not want anyone in our new "middle-class" neighborhood to know what was really going in our household. When I saw this, I quickly retreated to my bedroom upstairs as usual whenever he would carry on with his insane antics. Many times my mom took the place of that rotary phone.

As I mentioned before, our house was an alternate universe where my father was the dictator. But within this alternate universe, I managed to create my own alternate world. I lived there and later on so did my little sister, who I will call Natalie and baby brother, Nash.

My bedroom was a refuge. I shared it with Natalie who is eight years younger. At this time, I was 12 and she was 4. It was here in our room that we would hide underneath the bed or between the bed and the far wall by the window and read a huge illustrated children's Bible that our mother bought for us. This book was bigger than both our heads put together. I would try to read the verses with my sister with exaggerated feeling so that she would feel like she was away for a moment in Ancient Bible times, away from our father without having to physically run away. I knew I was doing okay when she would follow along with me and smile and laugh. I didn't understand most of what I was reading but it sure sounded good. I prayed that God would help me to understand one day.

My father was an atheist, but strange enough, he was alright with us celebrating religious holidays. There was a disclaimer though. As he would put it,

"I am Santa Clause. I am the Easter Bunny. I am the Tooth Fairy and I am god."

Thus, we wouldn't make the mistake of giving thanks to any of these. All acknowledgements for any gifts that he gave us should go to him implicitly. This is the way things were.

On the flipside, my father would always mail holiday and birthday cards to Natalie and I and it was always so exciting receiving them in our mail box. He would time the mail so well that every year on my birthday, my birthday card would be delivered on that day. If my birthday fell on a Sunday, it would come that Saturday. I really felt special. Strange enough, my father always knew how to make me feel special.

I was a torn child. I saw my father do and say such mean, nasty and ridiculously insane things, yet, he was my daddy and I loved him. He would take the time out to teach me things. He would ride me around New York City and the surrounding boroughs giving me an educated tour of landmarks, important buildings etc. He always had aspirations of me becoming a doctor and living a more privileged life than he did so he always pushed me to be all that I could be in school. So when my mother asked me the week of her death, "Who would you like to live with if your daddy and I got a divorce?"

I panicked at just the sheer thought of being away from my father and I said,

"I don't want you to get a divorce. I want to be with the both of you."

Sometimes, even now, I regret saying that. I wonder if I said, "I want to be with you", what the outcome would have been. Would she still be alive? But I have to consciously force myself to remember that I was just a child and all children want their parents to be together regardless of the difficulties that exist when they are together.

Children as well as adults, have a way of adapting to dysfunctional relationships. I believe this is the instinct in all of us to survive. Desperation to live becomes a motivating factor. We get so used to the same thing that we forget what "normal" is. When we are fortunate enough to be removed from our toxic environment, initially, we don't know how to act in the new, better situation. We sometimes long to be back in the old abusive state. Then, with time and counseling, we get used to the new, better situation as well. We are creatures of habit and although the initial change is awkward, we eventually learn to adapt. But as kids, we don't go through these thought processes. We just want everything to be right - and right is having both mommy and daddy together.

By the time I was six years old, I had already witnessed scenes between my parents that not even an adult should have to be exposed to. When I was five years of age, my father was slapping my mother around as usual as she begged for him to stop. I was probably no more than 3 ½ feet tall as I watched these mammoth people stumble from room to room. The assault spread all over our apartment but it ended in the living room. My tiny heart almost beat out of my chest and my breath hastened with fear. They did not see me following them. At this point, I could see the sweat glistening off my father's bare back. As they burst into the living room, my father pushed my mom on to our red and gold living room couch covered in plastic and proceeded to tear her clothes off. I stopped in my tracks in the kitchen but I couldn't take my eyes off of my parents. I didn't understand what was going on but I knew it wasn't good. I could smell the fear from my mother and the anger from my father. She tried to fight him off but she was no match for his brute strength. Chills took over my whole body and left me frozen, watching from the kitchen. I wanted to help but I couldn't and I felt so bad that I couldn't protect my mommy. I will always remember her screaming for him to stop and the three scratches she left on his back.

I didn't realize what exactly occurred until I was about 10 or 11 years old when I learned about the "birds and the bees" from school peers. I have had plenty of "dawning moments" such as this as I reached my teenage years and beyond, where the full reality as to what I was actually witnessing as a child, became clearer. Then it's like reliving the whole thing all over again, but with more intense feelings. It's like Adam and Eve after eating from the tree of the knowledge of good and bad, having their eyes opened and realizing they were naked. Were they better off in the mind set when they were naked or when they saw the need to clothe themselves?

Chapter Three

MY BEST FRIEND FOREVER

GROWING UP SEEING THE FIGHTS, the bruises, hearing the crying and cursing and screaming, there was a need for imagination. With pencil in hand and a blank, white paper staring at me, I discovered my best friend forever. My best friend has no gender and can not be seen by mere eyes. It is felt and through it I have gotten through the worst of times. My BFF is writing. I discovered my ability to write fictional stories at the age of five. I realized that I could travel anywhere and be anything I wanted to be when I put pencil to paper, allowing my imagination to soar. This defense mechanism I seemed to have developed created a way for me to take a deep breath and let my mind relax from the chaos. It was and still is my best friend. When I feel stressed, I write and this certainly lessens the anxiety. As a child, when my father would attack my mother, I would slink back into my room, pull out my favorite composition notebook and just write about being somewhere else. I could literally block out the yelling and screaming as I delved deeper into the story at hand.

I remember my first story book. I scotch-taped ten white ruled index cards with two plain blue ones for the front and back cover. The name of the story was, "The Wolf, The Fox and the Four Children." I drew the four children and their mother on the front cover in pencil. The story was about a fox and a wolf that tried to hunt down and eat four children as they looked for nuts and berries for dinner as their mother instructed them to. They were poor and thanks to the forest, these were the delicacies that they could have for free. The children ran for their lives but then one of them, out of breath and tired of running, stopped and asked, "Why are we running from the wolf and the fox?" The other children stopped too and looked at each other, enlightened, "Yeah. Why are we running from them?" From this point, they devised a plan to outsmart the wolf and the fox and they succeeded to trap them. Along with their nuts and berries, that night, they also had wolf soup and fox stew. It was a happy ending.

As I look back now, I think the fox and the wolf depicted my father (especially since a father figure is not present in the story). I, like one of the kids, got tired of running from him, or running from his dysfunction, so I saw the need to outsmart him. I think that I outsmarted him in that although I was stuck in the house physically, I wasn't stuck psychologically. My imagination kept reminding me that there existed a better way of life; a free place where I could be happy and not spend my time having to prepare myself for the next outburst. My stories gave me power over my life and made me feel whole. For this reason, I call the ability to write my imagination onto paper and find real comfort in it, my oldest and dearest friend – My BFF.

Fortunately, this ability to write also benefited me greatly in school. On citywide tests, I always placed in the 90+ percentile. Once, in grade school, I received a 99% score on one of these comprehensive tests. The summary of the tests would always have the same short explanation of my grade – able to read the New York Times newspaper with understanding. While writing reports and essays were not my cup of tea, they still turned out to be very well written, so much so, that my fifth grade teacher accused me of cheating by having an adult write my take home book report. I did not make a fuss. I actually saw this as a compliment. 'Wow.' I thought. 'She really loves the way I write.' Ms. Kora made me sit down alone in class that same day, while my classmates enjoyed their lunch break in the cafeteria, and read a short story and then write a report on it. When I was done, she took it and dismissed me. She never told me how I did and I never asked her being the shy, quiet girl that I was. Nothing was ever said about it after that day. I took her unresponsiveness to mean that I did well.

I couldn't let my father know about this because he would have marched up to the school and made a big fuss the very next day. Looking back, I should have told him but back then, I was embarrassed every time he would show up at the school to protest. One day he noticed that I was doing homework on the theory of Evolution. He showed up at the school the next day in the Principal's Office to make a complaint about having Evolution as part of the curriculum. He refused to allow me to be taught that I originated from primates. "My child did not originate from monkeys!" He would say.

The end result was that my teacher herself burst into tears in front of us because she did not agree with the curriculum as well and had been fighting with her conscience to simply do her job.

In another incident, a substitute teacher made my class, the honors class of the 6th grade write for homework 500 times, *I will not make noise on the stairwell.* When my father saw my homework, he showed up to the school the next morning to complain about the sub. He said in part, very firmly to everyone in the Principal's Office, "I will not allow my daughter to hurt her fingers writing mindless sentences when she could be using her fingers to write something of substance. Is this what this school is teaching her?!"

Well, we never had that substitute teacher again. If nothing else, I did respect my father for always checking my homework thoroughly and taking a proactive stance with regard to my education.

To this day it confounds my mind. How could a man who seemed to love his children so much, hate their mother?

Chapter Four

MY FAVORITE AUNTIE

AUNTIE ABIGAIL WAS MY FAVORITE Auntie. She was and still is a tough cookie. But one day when she came over to our home when I was about four or five years of age, all of her tough exterior melted like butter on hot coals in the matter of a second.

My father was always fascinated with guns. He would buy toy guns for me to play with and he would collect real guns for himself. Apparently, I watched where he stashed a particular silver looking gun with a white handle. This is the same gun that I would watch my father threaten my mother with, putting it to her head over and over again, as she pleaded with drenched eyes for him to stop. This made him feel powerful I guess. How pitiful, but I digress.

I must have thought this gun to be intriguing in some way. Maybe it was because it was so shiny. At any rate, Auntie Abigail, who was around sixteen at the time, sat down on a little chair of mine, playfully teasing me as she normally would. This time though, I pushed a chair against my parent's Chest of Drawers, climbed up to the top drawer and pulled out my father's shiny silver gun. Auntie Abigail told me that, she didn't see me coming. All she felt was the revolver against her temple and she froze in time. Her body became cold and stiff and she couldn't even move her mouth to call my mom for help from the kitchen. She was afraid that any little movement on her part would make me to pull the trigger.

When my mother finally came into the bedroom, she was completely and utterly mortified. What kind of scene that must have been. Can you imagine seeing your toddler pointing a gun at your teenaged sister's head? A toddler who thought it was just another toy like the ones daddy would usually buy her.

Unknowingly, my father was already teaching me a most horrific lesson; a lesson that could have ended up landing me in jail as a juvenile delinquent later on in life or probably a career criminal with a rap sheet starting at the age of four if I didn't have the proper guidance from my mother, her family and more importantly, God. My father was teaching me that if someone made me angry, shoot them. He didn't have to sit me down and give me the rundown of the lesson plan. I simply learned from his example.

Children are what I call, Genius Sponges. They suck in everything around them at a remarkable rate and their memories rival that of computers. Therefore parents, do not think that your children don't know your patterns. Their heightened awareness allows them to record and imitate your every move and everything that comes out of your mouth. Children observe everything so please be as good as an example to your children as you can be. And please do not expose them to bad television or your bad behavior. We all get mad at times but let's not give our children a front row seat to the horror show.

Be that as it may, my mother thought quickly and grabbed the gun from my hand. It was loaded.

Chapter Five

THE EMPATH

"**I**DON'T WANT TO LEAVE BECAUSE of the kids." This is a statement that most persons in abusive relationships repeat. This justification not to act and leave is wearing thin though. Many persons have died using it. Granted, children naturally want their parents to stay together no matter what. They feel broken inside when the two halves of who they are, are separated. But imagine how broken a child feels each time they witness the abuse. Imagine for a moment how broken a child will be when they are burying one parent and the other is locked away in prison for their murder. Imagine them dead.

Some adults feel a degree of empathy for others but children are natural empaths. They are extraordinarily sensitive to everything that goes on around them, especially when it comes to someone they love dearly. Unknown to my father, I felt all of my mother's pain. I can't tell you how many times I have seen my father beat my mother to a pulp in front of me. It didn't matter how much she tried to fight back, he would over power her with heavy punches as if he were beating another man.

My father had the habit of pretending to hug my mother (in a head lock) in front of me and with a smile on his face, he would watch me and give her upper cuts to the gut and ribs as if I didn't have two eyes to see. Every time he punched her, he was punching me. Every time he kicked her, he was kicking me. Every time he slapped her around, called her derogatory names and told her she was worthless, it felt as though he was doing all of these things to me. I remember in the Bible when God delivered the Jews from Babylon he said to them, "He that is touching you is touching my eyeball"- Zechariah 2:8. This is how sensitive I was to my mother's pain.

After a beating, to add more insult to injury, my father would look at me and say in front of mom, "Don't be like your mother. Do you hear me?!" I would watch my mother walk away with her head down, ashamed. The physical pain was nothing compared to the worthlessness and utter self hatred she felt. Although I started out life chipper and full of energy and confidence, my diabolical family life made sure that I soon became shy and introverted. Like my mother, I developed a self-loathing. By the time I was about 10 years of age, I couldn't look at myself in the mirror. I thought I was ugly and disgusting and of course, I contemplated suicide. I remember banging my reflection in the mirror once because I hated myself so. I wanted to break it but I knew I would get in trouble, so I didn't.

What I really want victims to understand is that children are very empathetic. They pick up everything you are experiencing, the good and the bad. You are in danger of losing your children emotionally and your children are in danger of losing you if you stay in the abusive situation. It is not easy to pick up and go but there are many programs and organizations that are specifically designed to help you and your family leave. I wish many of the programs that exist today, existed when my mom was alive.

Chapter Six

DIAMONDS IN THE STREET

ONE FALL MORNING, I TREKKED to school down my usual route. With my huge back pack bopping against my back, I knew I would be there in less than ten minutes since I only lived three blocks away. As I turned the corner I saw something amazing. The street up ahead was sparkling in the soft morning sunlight. I had to find out what was causing this so I hurried to get closer. Lo and behold my 7 year old eyes saw diamonds; hundreds of diamonds littered all over the street. What I didn't know was that this phenomenon was really the remnants of a very bad accident that must have occurred early that morning or the night before. A few cars drove by and I thought they must not be seeing what I was seeing or else the drivers would be jumping out of their cars, taking as many as they could. I peered sneakily to my left and then to my right to make sure no one would see me. Then with quick precision, I picked up a handful of the "diamonds" and pushed them in my pockets.

I didn't tell any of my friends or my teacher what I found that morning just in case they would try to take them from me. I went through the entire day, day dreaming about my mom's reaction when she would see the diamonds I found in the street. I knew she would be sooooo happy and all I wanted was for my mommy to be happy.

When I got home, I ran to my mom and pulled out my treasures, holding them in both hands with a big, accomplished smile on my face.

"Look Mommy! Look what I found?!"

Without hesitation, she knocked them out of my hand and on to the floor.

"What are you doing with glass in your hands?!" She scolded me.

"But they're diamonds…"

"Its glass not diamonds! Don't' ever pick things up from the street again!"

My happy bubble burst. I really thought in my 7 year old mind that when she saw the "diamonds", she would bear hug me and be overwhelmed with absolute joy. I thought that with the "diamonds", my mother and father would finally be able to buy a house where we would live happily ever after.

As a mom, I understand my mother's immediate concern. She just wanted to protect me from getting hurt and I just wanted to do exactly what all children in violent households want to do – protect the abused parent from getting hurt by making everything better. I saw this stroke of luck. I really thought finding "diamonds" in the street as the key to my mom's true happiness. Although she said they were glass, I still believed them to be diamonds, so for several nights, I would stare at them in bed before I would drift away to sleep.

Chapter Seven

THE RUN AWAY

Not too long after the diamonds in the street episode, at the age of 7, I decided that I couldn't take it anymore. 'It?' you may ask. The constant fighting, the blow ups, the tip toeing on egg shells knowing that a flare up was going to occur but not knowing when exactly. I had enough.

One Saturday morning I woke up and saw that no one was home. I went into each room calling for mommy and daddy but they were nowhere to be found. I became anxious. What I didn't know was that my father had dropped my mother off to work, hoping I wouldn't wake up until he returned. My mother worked in the dietary department in a Nursing Home. Her shifts were 6am – 1pm or 11am – 7pm or sometimes both if she wanted to be paid double time. This particular morning she worked the 6am shift thus the reason why they were gone so early.

Be that as it may, I saw this as an opportunity to just leave. Leave all the stress of having to experience my mother's grunts and screams and my father's relentless blows to her torso. For the most part, he would beat her in that area and now I realize this was so that there would be no visible signs of abuse. As I mentioned before, I used to write myself into my stories while the fighting would happen so as to magically beam myself into another world. But sometimes, that wasn't enough.

This is why I loved school so much. School was the only place I would feel at ease and feel wanted and praised for my good grades. No one knew what I had to endure before I came to school and at the end of the day. And I wasn't going to let anyone know what was going on at home. I was very ashamed. So I had a smile on my face all throughout the day everyday. It wasn't a painted on smile. My smile was real because I was really happy at school. I remember one day, one of my classmates stopped me and said, "I wish I was like you. You're always so happy." If she only knew.

So here I was, packing this red tote an aunt gave me with a picture of all the flags of the world in the front, arranged like the flags at the United Nations building in the City. I can't remember what I placed in the bag, but knowing me, it was extra clothing and my red and black, compact Mario Brothers video game. I zipped it up, put on my jacket and walked out the first door of our apartment. I didn't know where I was going. All I knew was that I was leaving this place. As I walked down the dark hallway, with the old, dirt brown carpet and brown plastic "wooden" wall panels, toward the second and last door with my U.N. bag in my hand almost dragging the floor, I started to hear a fiddling at the locks.

I stopped in my tracks. The door opened, steadily spilling morning sunlight into the dusty hallway. My father looked at me perplexed as he pulled his key out of the lock. "Where are you going?"

I stared at him with doe eyes and silence. The silence lasted for a good couple of seconds. He then locked the door and simply led me back inside and not a word was said about it that day or any other day. That was weird.

All children in abusive households feel imprisoned as I did. Many run away like I almost did but then they become victims of abuse on the streets, be it as a member of a gang, as a prostitute, a drug abuser etc. It is such a sad circle and for this reason I want to help these children (who seem to be forgotten by society) to know that they have a place they can go to for help. This is why I have joined with the Purple Ribbon Council to head up a support group for children who have lost their parent(s) to domestic abuse called the "Butterfly Club" in Brooklyn, New York. My hope is that the pilot program is so successful, that it is adopted in every city in the U.S. until there is no more need.

Sometimes I wonder how long I would have lasted on the street as a skinny 7 year old girl carrying a bright red bag around. I know I wouldn't have gotten too far.

Chapter Eight

THE GREEN EYED MONSTER

M Y FATHER NEVER LAID A hand on me or my siblings. In fact, he would beat my mother for physically disciplining me. Twisted? Yes. My mother actually told me one day that if I ever revealed to my father that she hit me, the beatings would get worst. The threat was real and I was cornered from all sides. This is why I mentioned in one of my earlier entries that because the family was a dysfunctional one, the roles were all confused. My father was the terrorist, my mother was the crime victim and my assailant at times and I was the victim and fly on the wall. I forgive my mother for beating me because she was all screwed up from my father's brainwashing. Don't get me wrong, she did treat me like a loving mother for the most part, but sometimes, I was her competition.

My father would purposely give me attention that should be given to a wife. He would supply me with innumerable toys. He would take me on tours throughout NYC. He would even take me along with my mother to restaurants every single Valentines Day. Talk about a third wheel! My mother thought she had no say in the matter. My father would also call my mother derogatory names in front of me like, pig, dumb, dog, stupid, asshole. Then he would turn around to me with the advice, "Don't be like your mother you hear!"

My father created a Petri dish for jealousy to be bred and fed between the greatest most natural human bond in my opinion that exists: The relationship between mother and child. Now I see the situation clearly. HE was jealous of my mother – period. And he wanted to project this jealousy unto my mother.

My mom finished High School in her native country - Barbados, West Indies which boasts the highest literacy rate in the world. In order to complete your secondary and post-secondary schooling and receive a certificate of completion in the Caribbean, a student would have to pass a highly comprehensive test arranged by the CXC

(Caribbean Examinations Council) which is fashioned after the British educational system.

My mom wanted to get a High School diploma in the United States. I watched her study diligently after work while my father walked around her and called her "stupid", and "dumb ass" and all the other derogatory terms he could conjure up. He even told her she would never pass the test. Well, my mother tuned him out for once and passed those tests. When she told me the good news, I could see a light sparkle in her eyes that I never noticed before. My heart leapt for her, I was so proud.

She framed her diploma and hung it in our living room with great pride. Every time I passed, I would gaze at it like a work of art in a museum. But of course, my father took it down and threw it on the ground and told her that he didn't want that 'piece of garbage' in his house. She put it up again the next day and he took it down again and this time he returned to physically beating her. I didn't see her put it up again after that. My mom and I knew it was there though. It would always be there.

I know for a fact that my father and other abusive insignificant others are jealous of the persons they are abusing. There is something about them that they wish they possessed. It could be as simple as their happiness that they covet.

If my mother were alive today, she would say, "What? Jealous of me?"

But yes. She couldn't see through her cloud of self-hatred (manufactured by my father) that she was worth so much. So much so she was priceless. She really thought she wasn't worth anything because my father reprogrammed her into thinking that she wasn't.

All of God's creations are worth something. We are so valuable that we are priceless! Don't let anyone try to make you believe that you are not. Hold your head up high and believe within yourself that you are priceless. This is the only way you can make that move by any means and leave the abusive situation.

Right now, I love myself for everyone who doesn't love me. People don't have to love you, but they will have to respect you for the love that you have for yourself. If they do not respect you, they do not respect themselves, thus they do not deserve to be in your presence. Believe that! The love that you have for yourself will transcend throughout your life and without a doubt, it will cause some to be jealous, but give them up to their jealousy from a distance because from my experience, they find ways to try to make you insecure and hate yourself as they do. Misery loves company.

Chapter Nine

DR. CHASE NERVE PILLS

I HAD MY FIRST "EMOTIONAL BREAKDOWN" when I was about 7 or 8. Every time I think about it, my heart races, I shudder and I shake as if I am there again. The incident wasn't unlike any other incident I witnessed before but I believe it was a culmination of all previous incidents of seeing my father abuse my mother that set me off.

It was a weekday and my mom and I were at my grandmother's house, spending some time with her. We laughed at the kitchen table as my grandmother's husband chimed in now and then in between being zoned out by his little television which sat on the counter in front of him all day. We waited for my father to pick us up. This was before my mother bought her own car.

The phone rang and we got our belongings together. We said our good byes and sped to my father's little grey Mustang which he treasured. He didn't like to be kept waiting. He didn't open the door for my mom or me as a gentleman would. He just sat in his seat. As soon as we stepped in, he started yelling at my mom. I can't remember what he was upset about but whatever it was, it didn't warrant him to start choking my mother in a headlock as he beat his knuckles into her forehead.

I sat in the back about three feet away, buckled into my seat. I couldn't close my eyes, or do anything for that matter to pretend this wasn't happening. My mother kept screaming his name, begging for him to stop but somehow this seemed to give him a boost of power and make him even angrier because he then took my mom's head and bashed it against the window over and over again. Her face turned red and she squeezed her eyes shut for every blow. His face had determination all over it; determination to knock the life right out of her. That was no longer my father. That was the face of a murderer.

I couldn't unbuckle myself fast enough. I had to get away and save my mom. I pushed the back door open, leaving it swinging and ran up the stairs to my grandmother's house. My mom cried out for me to come back but that wasn't happening. I rang the bell over and over and over again. My finger was in pain but I could not stop ringing it. Even when my grandmother and my Auntie Abigail ran to the door, I kept ringing it. My aunt pulled me into the foyer, kneeled down to my level and begged, "What happened?! What happened?!"

I couldn't speak. I opened my mouth but words couldn't come out. I desperately wanted the words to come out so someone could help my mom but they just wouldn't come out.

"Stop shaking Nicole and tell me what happened!" My aunt said peering over the walls of the porch.

Auntie Abigail took her hands and held both my arms together to stop me from shaking. I didn't even realize I was shaking until she told me to stop. Now I couldn't speak and I couldn't stop shaking.

"Where is your mommy?" My grandmother asked franticly.

Then I found words. But they were chopped up words, trying to escape through chattering teeth.

"D-d-d-d-a-d-d—y needs t-t-t-o b-b-be beaten a-a-and…and…"

Then Auntie Abigail interjected when she saw how painful it was for me to speak let alone recap the horrors I must have just seen.

"…And thrown in the garbage right?" She said with a smile on her face that was meant to comfort me.

"Ya-ya-ya-Yes!"

How did she know what I was feeling at that moment? Why didn't anyone go downstairs to help my mother? Why didn't anyone call the police? Was this all really normal and was I the only one who was crazy? All of these questions bounced against each other in my head like atoms in a rogue molecule. I had a headache, I couldn't stop shaking and my heart kept beating like a drum against my chest. The constant leaping of my heart made me feel faintish.

My aunt led me into the house again and there I stayed for a while until the shaking finally stopped. Then my grandmother came to me and told me that my mother and father wanted to see me. I was apprehensive, making tiny fearful steps out onto the porch. I saw them sitting halfway down the steps together.

"Come Nicole." My mom patted the space on the step next to her.

I moved cautiously like a cat in the wild.

"Your daddy will not hurt mommy like that again, okay."

I looked at her face and I could tell that she didn't believe her own words. She just wanted me to believe. I was too afraid to look at him. Then I heard his voice.

"I love your mommy very much. I'm sorry I hurt her."

Somehow his words sounded sincere. I loved my father very much but I didn't love the way he treated my mother. How I felt for him brought me much guilt. When he said that he loved her very much, I believe he believed that. But you don't pummel the one you love. For the moment, I felt at ease. I needed to feel ease. I needed a release. In the back of my mind, I knew this wasn't going to be the last round but I didn't want to think about that, so I didn't.

From this night on, every time my father would beat my mother up, my body would shake beyond my control. Even for a long time after everything settled, my body would take its time to settle again.

Trembling would become a regular occurrence for me. When I would pick up my pencil to write at school, I would curiously watch my hand vibrate like the pin in a lie detector test. I have broken many pencil points and many vinyl records have been scratched in my attempts to place the needle down precisely at its edge. I always started the song way past the beginning. I would try over and over again to place the needle down perfectly until I finally got it right.

Wine glasses would break in my hands as I tried to wash them. My mother saw the need to wash the glassware herself. She also saw the need to have me treated for my shaking fits somehow.

One day she called me into our kitchen when I was about 8 years of age and presented me with two brown over-the-counter pills. They looked like candies and they even tasted like candy on the surface. My mom explained to me that they were for my nerves and they would help stop me from shaking. I would chew two Dr. Chase Nerve Pills every morning before breakfast for a stretch of several months at the beginning and then for the next couple of years only when I had really uncontrollable episodes. My mother would take these pills as well. The whole Dr. Chase Nerve Food collection of "remedies" were first put on the market in the late 1800's and claimed to conquer ailments such as "Tired Feelings, Sleeplessness, Nervous Indigestion, Nervous Headache, Dizziness and Fainting", etc. I don't think they ever worked because I still remember shaking and having a difficult time sleeping at night.

Recently I decided to investigate these nerve pills and was surprised to find out that the original blend contained Strychnine and Arsenic. Both are very toxic poisons used as pesticides, particularly for killing small vertebrate such as birds and rodents. Arsenic is also used as an insecticide and herbicide. Why would poisons be an ingredient in a "remedy" that is supposed to cure a variety of human ailments. Apparently, strychnine and arsenic in very small doses were used as laxatives in the past until the Food, Drug and Cosmetic Act of 1938 outlawed them. But Dr. Chase Nerve Pills are still sold in the West Indian community and other ethnic populations in the United States and abroad. I am not sure if strychnine and arsenic are still present in Dr. Chase's Nerve Pills today but there is something to be said about a brand that is only sold in small bodegas as opposed to a pharmacy and on peculiar websites on the internet.

Of strychnine, the CDC notes, "Strychnine prevents the proper operation of the chemical that controls nerve signals to the muscles. The chemical controlling nerve signals works like the body's off switch for muscles. When this off switch does not work correctly, muscles throughout the body have severe, painful spasms. Even though the person's consciousness or thinking are not affected at first (except that the person is very excitable and in pain), eventually the muscles tire and the person can't breathe."

I don't know if this ingredient was in my daily doses of Dr. Chase Nerve Pills, but if it was, it would explain my constant muscles aches starting at the age of 8. I suffered throughout the day but mostly at night with pain radiating throughout my arms and legs. Sometimes the pain would attack both my arms alone or both legs or one leg and one arm. I used to tie the limb that was hurting with a rubber band or a long thick sock before I went to bed at night. This would lessen the pain but of course I know now that I was slowing down blood circulation to those limbs. When my mom noticed what I was doing one evening, she yelled at me to stop. I did for that night, but the pain was too unbearable so of course, I didn't listen.

Nevertheless my mother took me to the doctor. I don't know if he was a specialist or not but after several blood tests, I remember him saying that the pain was all in my head. I guess because he didn't have a "Pain-O-Meter", I had to be making it all up. I must hand it to my mother, when I had a problem, she would always seek out a second opinion. For example, two years later at age ten, I started to experience Thelarche, or my first breast bud in my left breast. The soreness was intense so my mom took me to a doctor. Right after examining me physically, his diagnosis was, "She has a tumor in her left breast. We will have to operate right away and give her a mastectomy before the cancer spreads."

My mom rushed home and called everyone she knew, frantic. Next thing I knew, I was seeing another doctor for a second opinion. After some tests, he came back and said with a smile on his face, "This is not a tumor. Your daughter's breast is simply beginning to grow, the first sign of puberty. It is normal for one breast to grow before the other. The soreness is normal too but don't worry, it is only temporary. Who is the doctor that gave you the cancer diagnosis?"

So now, with regard to my muscle pain, my mother took me to another doctor. This doctor's diagnosis was Rheumatoid Arthritis. My mother was stunned because no one in the family had Rheumatoid Arthritis and more importantly, she thought I was too young to be stricken with such a disease. The doctor told her that I must have been born with it. She wasn't satisfied with that diagnosis either so we went to another doctor for a third opinion. I love my mom! The third doctor's diagnosis was, Stress. "Extreme stress can cause physical pain with no known physical cause." I believe my mom was "satisfied" with that diagnosis because I don't remember receiving any treatment for Rheumatoid Arthritis and I don't remember any talk of me having Rheumatoid Arthritis after that. I just remember when the second doctor proclaimed it. And more importantly, we didn't go for a 4th opinion.

Stress came out on top as the winner. I can understand why Stress is called the "Silent Killer". There is no instrument to measure levels of stress but it is the underlying cause of most ailments, from Heart Disease to Asthma. I was diagnosed with asthma as an adult but I believe I had it since childhood. It just got worst with time. My asthma is brought on by an allergic reaction to airborne allergens given off by trees, dust and some animals such as cats, dogs and chinchillas.

As a treatment, my mom would give me baths in Epsom Salts or oatmeal. Before bed, she would rub my body down with Florida Water or Alcolada. These products are like liquid versions of Vicks, mentholated liquids. They gave me temporary relief and temporary relief was always greater than none at all.

Dr. Chase Nerve Pills, Epsom Salts, Chamomile, Florida Water and Alcalada – Plasters for the sore. Why trim a weed and leave the root? My mom knew very well the reason why I trembled and the reason why my muscles hurt. She knew that the best "remedy" for me would be to remove me from our dysfunctional, abusive household away from my father.

As a mother, I can now understand the internal turmoil she must have been putting herself through. I say "putting herself through" because it wasn't unnecessary. I can understand the fear of my father. She probably blamed herself for being his victim time and time again and I'm quite sure she blamed herself for the emotional and physical pain that I was experiencing. What loving parent would give birth to their first child and be content with them witnessing the abuse I did?

My mom felt as if she was in a prison, being held against her will. My father reveled in the knowledge that she was his slave; caged by his abusive words, his punches, his slaps, his kicks. The fact that this prison was without physical bars did not matter. The bars were psychological, brought on by my father's brainwashing scheme to make my mom feel like a piece of nothing. People never understand why a woman or man, victimized by Domestic Abuse, has such a hard time leaving. Fear is the reason. Fear is crippling. Fear is the prison. This is why I have learned to be fearless because I believe in Freedom.

Chapter Ten

ESCAPE

MY MOTHER TRIED TO ESCAPE my father on a number of occasions. I remember some scattered details of two of these incidents but fortunately, my maternal grandmother has filled in the blanks for me. I remember my mother waiting for my father to go to work one morning. As soon as he stepped out the door, she started packing franticly. A couple of her brothers came over and helped us move to my grandmother's house. It was a collaborative mission that was successful – for a time.

I was about 4 or 5 years of age (not long after I put my father's loaded gun to my aunt's head). I have memories of living at my grandma's house intermittently. I think we stayed there for about a school year because I remember going to kindergarten in her neighborhood. I found out as I got older that my father convinced my mom that he would commit suicide if she didn't return home. My father worked for the New York City Transit Authority and the train tracks were readily accessible to him. He claimed that he would electrocute himself by jumping on the third rail. My mom, being the big-hearted human being that she was, didn't want that on her conscience so she made the decision to go back to him although her mother and the rest of the family advised her not to.

The second time my mother left my father, it was a similar process of last minute packing and running. We ended up by grandma's house again. I always felt safe by grandma's house. There were always a lot of people there. It was kind of like a bed & breakfast & dinner for family in need. Our bedroom was large and used to belong to my mother's two younger sisters. Huge black and gold high school cheerleading pom poms that belonged to one of them, Aunt Celeste, still hung on the inside of the closet door. A card board multiplication table that my mom made for me the last time I was there, was still hanging on the outside.

I was 6 years of age at this time and attending first grade not far from the house. We stayed for another school year until my father got another bright idea. For some reason, I have no memory of this, but apparently my father took me from school one day without my mother knowing – Kidnapping. The school day wasn't over and he never picked me up before because my mom was separated from him. In those days, there were no strict rules regarding school pick up as there are now. He just said he was my father and I was released to him. Next, my father called my mom and told her that he was on the way to the airport with me. If she didn't come back to him, he threatened to take me away so she would never see me again. So, of course, my mother agreed to return to him and that was the end of everything. I wouldn't live at "grandma's bed & breakfast & dinner" again until 9 years later when my father ultimately murdered my mom.

The things that my father did were all attempts at control. No human should have control over another human being and no one should feel forced to be in a relationship with someone, especially not someone who definitely needs psychological help. There are more programs available today than there were two decades ago when my mother was in need. I took advantage of a couple of those programs to make sure that my ex stayed away from me. Don't be afraid. Stand up for yourself and your family and take that step. Escape to safety, peace of mind - Freedom.

Chapter Eleven

$100 BILLS

I ALWAYS KNEW THAT ONE OF my parents would die by the hands of the other. So from the age of 7, I would pretend now and then, that one of them died and I would go through the motions of extreme grief and sadness. My imagination would actually put me there, in the funeral parlor, as if my mom or dad was in the coffin, dead. I would cry and cry and the despair would envelope me until it stopped. Sounds weird, I know. But I actually made a conscious resolve in my head as a young child that I would prepare my mind for the inevitable so that when it did happen, it wouldn't hurt so much.

How did I know one of my parents would die by the hands of the other? It wasn't mathematics. They fought constantly, with my father having the upper hand always.

Actually, my mother would try to defend herself from the physical blows my father would plague her body with. Her skin would become raised with big red blotches everywhere, except for her arms and face of course. And her eyes would be filled with tears that welled up but never trickled out, at least not for me to see. Shame was written all over my mom's face as she looked at me every time my father would finish beating her.

When I was 6, we moved from a 2nd floor apartment in a two family house to the basement of another two family house one block away. I hated this place because it was dark and the windows were so little, I couldn't even climb out of them if I wanted to. So there was hardly any sunlight and the walls were 70's plywood panels. I still have an aversion to plywood panels. Every time I see them I am absolutely disgusted.

No matter how much my mom cleaned, the place would always smell like a garage, damp and rocky. At this home of ours, my mother showed me an envelope filled with $100 dollar bills for the first time. I can't remember how many bills were there exactly but it was a thick envelope. She sat me down as if she was giving me, "The

Talk". In my world, this was, "The Talk"- instructions on how to save my life when she died.

"I am putting this envelope under my mattress. If anything happens to me, take it and go to your grandmother's house." She told me.

I was either 7 or 8 at the time and I knew exactly what she meant by "If anything happens to me...", so I just shook my head in agreement. Back then, it felt chilling but normal. Now I wonder, 'How the hell can $100 bills compensate for the loss of my mother? What was she thinking?'

But she wasn't thinking. My mom was feeling; feeling pure desperation, knowing that her life was on the line every single day.

I want everyone in abusive relationships and environments to understand that they can get help. There are many programs that can help you regardless of how trapped you may feel. There is no reason for anyone to live in fear for their life. Save your children, save yourselves!

The next time we moved, it was into our house. Our own house! My parents bought a beautiful 3 bedroom home with a huge backyard, cute front lawn and a full basement. I was 10 at this time and so elated to have a big bedroom to myself. Then my mom came to me again with Part II of, "The Talk". She showed me a thick envelope full of $100 bills and said, "If anything happens to me, take this, okay."

Somehow I thought that moving into this house was going to mean change for the better. Maybe, I thought, my father would stop beating my mother and we could be like those families on TV. But when my mother came to me with the same low, secretive voice (although my father was out somewhere) and showed me that envelope again, this time with even more $100 bills, I sighed inside my soul. At that moment I realized, we weren't transitioning to a better place at all.

Dismayed I complied, "Okay mommy".

Then she stuffed the envelope underneath the carpet in her bedroom by the closet door in the corner. Six years later, when my father finally did kill my mom I totally forgot about the envelope filled with $100 bills. I was only concerned about saving myself, and the lives of my little brother and sister.

Chapter Twelve

SIGNS AND THE IMAGINATION

WHEN I TOLD MY YOUNGER sister about this book and explained to her how therapeutic it was writing about my past experiences with our parents, she brushed over it lightly. I knew she didn't really want to know the details of what I knew about our family life. She has heard stories told from other relatives but not really from me. From the time she was born, I made a resolve at the age of 8 that I would protect her by any means necessary from the atrocities that I had to witness. So when I sensed that a blow- up was about to occur, I would remove her from the situation.

I was already programmed to know when a fight would break out. I would see the "signs". Late at night on the weekends, my father would come home drunk, decked out in his slobbering binge drinking regalia. This was almost always a recipe for disaster. He might silently stare at my mom with the flickering fire of ill intent in his eyes. This was a sure sign that an eruption was about to occur. Or he would go out of his way to create a totally pointless argument. As I mentioned before, he would occasionally (when my mother was home before him) come home from work and feel the vintage yellow rotary phone on the wall in the kitchen to see whether it was warm or cold. If it was warm, that meant my mother was talking on it with her friends, and this "horrid act" was forbidden.

If she truly was speaking on the phone and heard my father's keys in the door or the garage door opening, I would watch her jump up immediately, rush off the phone and head upstairs to appear busy with some household activity like separating laundry or tailoring his clothes. Sadly, my mom was trained like one of Pavlov's dogs. When he felt the warmth of the phone, that was an automatic argument and almost always grounds for a beating. Everyday I felt as if I was watching a bad movie that had no ending and the worst part was that there was no way of escaping the theater. As a child, I would actually pretend that my life was just a movie, not reality. A made for television movie where as the season ended with the last day of school and began again with the first day of school. In the morning, as I would hop to school, I would sing the theme song which would be some popular song that I fancied at the moment.

Anyway, when I would see the signs, I would move my sister to another room and engage her in some creative play with our many toys; something fun that would distract her. I even transformed our once dusty, box-ladened basement into a Playland/Classroom. Our father brought home a huge two-tiered wooden desk that we used to botch experiments with our chemistry set. He said he made it but I knew he didn't because he certainly was not a handy man. Nevertheless, we were happy to have it. A paper map of the world hung behind it on the wall so that desk also served as a news casting desk. I used my father's huge video camera to tape these *broadcasts*.

We played chess on a large glass board inlayed in thick pine wood (which he also said he made). This board also doubled as a dance floor for the Barbie dolls. The dolls were our actors to many of our off the wall soap operas and talent shows.

My mother topped off the basement with a fluffy cream-colored carpet on which we would make snow angels and roll around pretending it was snow. The two clothes lines above served as ski lifts for the Barbies. In that basement, I taught my sister how to read before she even started school, just as my parents taught me. Reading was essential in order to delve deeply into the pleasantly distracting world of the imagination. Although my father forbid me from reading anything fictional, I made sure to introduce my sister to the literary land of fiction starting with my favorite books, _Ira Sleeps Over_ and _Where the Wild Things Are_ and, of course, Shakespeare whose works I love. She became an avid reader of everything and right now her literary resume is tremendous, spanning all throughout the classics and beyond.

So when I mentioned my memoir to Natalie, I knew it wouldn't be on her to do list of works to delve into but I just thought I should make her aware of it. I brought one experience from it to her attention and my normally extremely talkative sister whose mouth my mother comically proclaimed 'ran like faucet water' and who she prophetically described as "the next Oprah Winfrey", went silent. She witnessed some of our parent's tamer fight scenes but there are some events that I screened her from that she is still not aware of to this day.

The rape incident stunned her into a silence so strange that I decided at that moment to continue to shield her from some things for her sake. Not everyone can handle hearing the grave details of abuse. Imagine the children forced to experience it first hand everyday.

Our imaginary winter wonderland in the basement was our great escape. There, our laughter painted the walls and our snow angels tattooed the carpet. This was our secret place of protection. Little did we know that our mother would later die there on the fluffy cream-colored carpet.

Chapter Thirteen

QUE SERA SERA

ONCE I REMEMBER MY FATHER yelling at the top of his lungs because my mom slightly burned a pot of rice. I sat in the living room as he began throwing insults and utensils at her in the kitchen. I was about 12 at this time and I didn't move as I usually would to a place of temporary refuge. Since we moved into our house two years earlier, I had not seen a fight. Not to say that they didn't happen, I just didn't see any and I started to get used to living a normal, more peaceful life. So there I sat, frozen on the living room sofa. I wanted with all my heart to rush into the kitchen and stab my father repeatedly until he stopped hurting my mommy. I wanted to stop him by any means necessary and at that moment, I felt capable. But this frightened me, so I sat frozen so I wouldn't do it. I had to endure hearing my mother's head knock against hard objects and her grunts as he was probably choking her as usual. Her will to fight back was bigger than usual but she was no match for the depth of my father's fury. I sat there shaking as I normally would, holding on to the edge of the sofa cushion so I wouldn't get up walk into that kitchen and do something I would regret.

Tired, my father stopped beating mommy and walked out of the kitchen as cool as can be with this bogus confident strut that sickened me. I watched him walk straight out the front door. Now I could finally exhale. The trembling didn't stop though. Then I heard something from the kitchen; familiar sounds that filled the air. I felt so awkward going around my mother after she was beaten because of a mix of emotions. She always looked defeated afterwards and I hated seeing her like that. I felt guilty because I always felt I should have done something to stop my father from hurting her. But as always, we pretended like nothing ever happened and went on with our regular business.

I tip toed to the kitchen and there she was, washing the dishes as if nothing happened and singing a tune she would usually sing after one of my father's blow ups. *'Que Sera, sera. Whatever will be will be.'*

My mother had a pretty, soothing voice and she would find herself singing and humming a tune all the time. If he was around, most likely he would yell at her to "Shut up!" as he's done on many occasions before. She wouldn't shut up immediately but with his persistence and threats to bash her face in, she would eventually stop. I found out some years later from childhood friends of my father's in Barbados that he would do the same thing to them when he was younger. If they sang, he would order them to shut up. If they didn't stop singing, he would beat them up. Why they continued being his friend even in adulthood is beyond me.

But anyway, since he stepped out this time, she could freely sing like a house wren in mid flight.

I wondered if my mom was simply singing a tune or if she felt the words to the song. Was she really so crushed to nothing that she made the twisted resolve in her mind that this was her life and that was it? Whatever will be, will be?'

Chapter Fourteen

NOVEMBER 22ND

I HAVE NOT WRITTEN ANYTHING IN any of my blogs for over a week now. Granted, affairs at work and at home have picked up a notch in the busy department but that has never stopped me from writing before. I did a momentary Zen-like pause yesterday and did some introspection, coming to the only plausible conclusion. The anniversary of my mom's death is creeping up. Like a natural law imbedded in my inner clock, the anniversary of her murder causes a reaction in me every single year. The same phenomenon happens to my sister who was 8 years old at the time. Usually we're depressed for a week or so. This year has been my busiest year for some reason and I haven't shed a tear as yet but that's not an indication that I'm not tortured inside anymore. And as far as my writing goes, I have not experienced that "Ah-ha" moment that would normally make me drop my twizzler and rush to my computer to write until 1:00 am. I'm forcing myself to write right now.

Tomorrow, November 22nd 2008, will be 17 years since my mother was murdered by my father. It feels like only one year has passed. Still fresh in my psyche are the details leading up to her death and the details directly after. It was a cold November Friday night. For the first time in the 6 years that we were living at our home, my father locked the only lock on the front door that everyone knew I didn't have a key for. It couldn't be locked without a key. My father was now a supervisor in New York City Transit and so his job, according to him, was to drive around in a van and make sure all his workers were doing what they were supposed to be doing. He used to come home for lunch on occasion, so he was the only one who had access to the house after I left for school.

When I came home from school, I was locked out. I headed over to my cousin's house just two houses away as my father probably estimated. My sister followed suit when her school bus dropped her off. We had fun playing around at my cousin's house. It was peaceful compared to ours. So as I looked through my cousin's bedroom window and saw my father pulling up in his car from work around 5pm, I did not go home. I wanted to stay where I was for as long as I could. He didn't even come over to get my little sister and I because this would get in the way of his plan. Time passed and when my mom arrived about 7:30 pm, with my little brother, my father was asleep. He didn't even hear the noisy garage door open. Mom came over to my cousin's house to collect my sister and me.

We entered our home to see my father just rousing from his nap. We took our coats off and dispersed. I went straight to the living room television in expectation of my mother's favorite show, ironically titled, "Family Matters". She affectionately called it "Erkyl" after the minor character who later became the main one. I remember my mom, rummaging through her coats in the closet, looking for Natalie's misplaced prescription for eyeglasses. Not too long after that, my father picked a senseless fight with my mom. I resigned to my bedroom upstairs as usual but as I found out later, Natalie started attacking my father as he attacked our mom. He pushed her away and continued to hammer into our mother. After he beat her up in our living room, my mother headed quietly down to the basement to do laundry as if nothing ever occurred. My little 3 year old brother was always with my mom, so he followed her down the stairs crawling backwards. My sister also followed her down there to protect her. I think the intention in their young minds was to make mommy feel better with their company. I, on the other hand, was bred in a more hostile environment, so I did what I did every time a blow up would occur. I vacated the premises. I stayed in my room until things quieted down. After 9:00 pm, I decided to go back downstairs. There I would witness a more horrific series of events.

As I sat there watching "Family Matters" in the living room by myself, I peeped my father reaching for his gun on the top shelf in the front coat closet. This is the same gun he showed me earlier that same week on Monday and told me, "If any of your mother's friends come here when I am not here, shoot them." I thought to myself, *He has finally lost it.* I did not answer him. After he placed the gun high up in the closet, he went to the kitchen with a coffee tin. He told me to come in the kitchen with him. We stood by the counter side by side. Then he uncovered the tin to reveal innumerable bullets with gold colored tips. I couldn't believe what I was seeing. My heart started jumping out of my chest but I couldn't let him think at that moment that I was against him. I acted like everything he was doing was normal and I tried really hard not to set him off by shaking. He said, "Use these bullets if you have to. The gun is loaded right now anyway."

When my mom came home that night, I told her every piece of craziness my father told me. "He put the gun in the closet Mommy!" I yelled. I don't know what was going through my mother's head. She started to smile and say, "Your father is just stupid."

I tried to inject some sense into her. "But mommy, he put the gun right there in the closet. You wanna see it?" She shook her head with the same strange smile on her face and said, "He would never use that."

I don't know if my mom was just trying not to get me riled up by her "couldn't care less" attitude but it freaked me out. I thought I had gone deeper into the depths of the "Twilight Zone" and my thinking was abnormal, and everything that I thought was weird was really normal.

Had she forgotten all the times he put the gun to her head? And what about all those times he threatened to kill her and pull the veil over her face in her coffin? Had she forgotten all of the beatings? Nothing made sense to me.

My father came home that Monday night as peaceful as can be but then he never came home the next night or the night after that. He has never slept out before. I don't know if my mom knew where he was but she didn't seem to be alarmed. She may have just been relieved. He showed up again on Thursday with no explanation; not to me anyway.

Here he was now, Friday night, with the gun from the closet in his hand, heading down to the basement. When he was out of sight, I immediately ran upstairs to the phone in my mom's bedroom. Then I thought quickly. 'Who should I call? The police? No! I got in trouble for that from my mother before. My grandmother? Yes!' (This was a decision that got me blamed by family members for my mother's death for a few years to come). While I waited for grandma to pick up the phone, I heard a loud commotion in the basement. They were definitely fighting. I heard my mother scream in frustration,

"If you're going to shoot me, go ahead and shoot me!" That's when I heard the shot. Then dead silence.

My grandmother repeated,

"Hello?! Hello?!"

In a daze I stated very plainly, "Daddy just killed mommy." My grandmother screamed, "What?! What's going on there Nicole?! What's going on?!..." At that moment, my father started to dial from the rotary phone in the kitchen downstairs. When he realized I was already on the phone he yelled at me to get off. In his frantic sounding words,

"Nicole, get off the phone now! I'm trying to call the cops. Something happened to your mother!"

I hung up the phone slowly, hearing the drifting screams coming from my grandmother. I floated downstairs to meet my brother and sister's blank faces at the foot of the steps. I told them to go up to my bedroom and they did quickly. I don't know why but something told me to go towards my father in the kitchen. I heard him telling a tale to the police as he usually did. On the way to the kitchen I stopped at the basement door because the yellow walls leading down were all covered in thick bloody hand prints. When I reached my father, I saw his hands smothered in bright red blood. The yellow rotary phone on the wall was now red. When he saw me, he hung up the phone and walked towards me. He stood next to me and watched me standing in that one spot, immovable, watching the bloodied walls. "Go downstairs and see what happened to your mother. Something happened to your mother", He said calmly.

Something told me not to go downstairs. I had a strong feeling that as I walked down those stairs, my father would shoot me in the back. He was standing right next to me on my left side with the gun held down in his right hand. I was staring at the blood and he was staring at me, waiting to see if I would go down. As much as I loved my father and as much as I know he loved me, I knew this man was going to shoot me once I turned my back and walked down those basement steps. He professed to love my mom, his wife of 17 years, and yet he just killed her. What would stop him from doing the same to me? Then, it seemed like some kind of force pulled him away from me and back to the yellow, bloodied rotary phone to call the police again.

I swear everything was occurring in slow motion. I myself moved slowly in order not to set my father off. I had to act like nothing just happened. He didn't just beat and shoot my mother to death. She wasn't lying in the basement bleeding out.

As he continued with his call, I went straight to the coat closet and grabbed my sibling's coats and shoes and headed upstairs. Although I told them to go in my room, they were just milling around in mommy's bedroom. I don't know if it was her smell or her essence that still lingered there but they were drawn to her bedroom. Well the whole room had her signature all over it, the plush burgundy carpet was picked out by her, the satiny bed spread, and the light beige curtains, flowers outlined in burgundy at the valence, were made by her. So I could see why they just stood there at the foot of her bed. They were in shock at what they had just seen.

I guided the two little ones to my bedroom. We really didn't interact verbally besides me telling my 8 year old sister to put her coat and shoes on fast. All the while, I extended my ear down to the kitchen to make sure my father was still distracted, on the phone. I told Natalie to go over to our cousin's house two houses away. My intention was to have at least one of us escape this hell and our father's wrath. I really didn't think my brother or I would survive this night. Like mice, my sister and I inched down the carpeted steps. Then I opened up the front door as slowly as possible because it had the habit of screeching with every move. At this point, my father wasn't at the phone anymore and I couldn't see him. He could have been in the basement again. I don't know.

My heart went with my sister as she trekked into the night over to our cousins. I thought about the danger of being outside at this time of night but then I estimated that the danger inside was far greater than what she could experience out there. At any rate, the house was only a few feet away. I closed the door slowly but not completely, and rushed upstairs to my baby brother. I bundled him up with his coat, hat and shoes and then I followed suit. I gathered him in my arms to head out but not after first peeking down the stairwell to pin point my father's whereabouts. He didn't seem to be around, so I hurried through the front door.

To my dismay, as soon as I stepped out the door, I could see my sister still standing on my cousins porch, in front of a locked door. Apparently, my cousin and her husband double locked the door as they always did at night and were searching for the key. I rushed over there with my brother in my arms as fast and quietly as I could. No one was outside on our block to ask for help. It was as if everyone was gone in the world and the three of us were the only ones left behind.

As I joined Natalie, my cousin came to the door.

"What happened?!"

"Can you please open the door?" I pleaded looking around.

"We're trying to find the key."

'Who locks themselves inside their house?' I thought to myself.

At that moment, my father came out of our house with his gun in hand, looking around screaming my name. "Nicole!!! Nicole!!!" He must have been searching for all of us in the house. For a moment, he looked dead in the direction of the three of us but he never saw us. He just kept on screaming my name with that gun in his right hand.

I held my little brother's mouth so he wouldn't make a sound and my sister already knew to stay quiet. Six enlarged terrified eyes, stared at my father. Three heart beats trembled uncontrollably. We just wanted to live.

Interestingly enough, there was no reason for our father not to see us. Our porch light was on and so was the house next door and our cousin's. Also, every house on the block had its own beautiful Holly Tree. Of all the features of our block, this was the one that gave it real character. So when our new next door neighbors cut down their Holly, we were mortified. "How could they kill something so beautiful? What's wrong with them?", we said. Even my father was against that decision. So that Friday night, there was nothing in my father's way that blocked him from seeing the three of us, huddled together, staring dead at him as he stared at us. When I first came out on my porch, I saw my sister standing there as plain as day. Why couldn't he? Without a doubt, I believe God protected us that night. There is no other explanation. God delivered all three of us from our father that night.

As we clustered together in front of our cousin's house, for what felt like an eternity, her husband finally returned to the door fiddling with the keys. He asked us what happened. I whispered and begged, "Please open the door." I looked back to see if my father, who now made his way down the path of our front lawn, heard me. I felt that he did. And he looked toward our direction. But at that moment, the door opened and we all rushed in like raging water through a broken dam. "Close the doors quick! Lock the doors!" I begged. Our cousin and her husband watched us in terror and asked us, "What Happened?!"

Finally I was able to release everything from the night that I had been holding in calmly as my mother lay dying in our basement. I felt like screaming an endless scream with my arms outstretched as if I were in the middle of the Grand Canyon. I put my brother down and in between asthmatic wailing and tears and more crying, the words finally came out. "Daddy killed Mommy."

My cousin's husband proclaimed that he was going to go over to see what happened. I advised him not to because my father had a loaded gun and lots of bullets. He still insisted and made his way over there. He found my father in the basement over my mother's body. Minutes after that, the police officers my father called, poured into our house and ordered both my father and my cousin's husband to the ground.

The police eventually spilled over into my cousin's home. All you could see was a sea of blue and speckles of suited men everywhere. The siren's kept blaring and the red and blue lights kept piercing through the living room window.

An officer brought my cousin's husband over to confirm his identity. Although my cousin was yelling, "That's my husband! That's my husband!" They only wanted my confirmation as the oldest witness to the murder. Although I didn't actually see the murder, I was present, so I was a key witness. I confirmed his identity and then they let him go.

A female officer was assigned to my siblings and I, of course. She sat us down and gently asked what happened. My little sister looked at me with tear drenched eyes, while everyone around us bustled back and forth. The first words that she spoke to me since she saw the murder were -

"Nicole...Why did daddy kill mommy?"

"I don't know Natalie. I don't know." That was all I could offer her.

I remember looking over at my 3 year old brother who couldn't speak as yet due to the traumatic environment he was subjected to. Silence descended and all I saw was one tear drop, stretched and trailing from his eye. His little face, complete with flushed pink cheeks, pleaded to me. At that moment, I felt him call me "Mommy". And I felt the child in me leave.

PART II

The Aftermath

Chapter Fifteen

WATER IS THICKER THAN BLOOD
SOMETIMES

"I'M GOING TO MAKE YOU guys rich!" This is exactly how one of my aunts, Aunt Celeste, greeted us when we finally left Police Precinct 69 and arrived at my grandmother's house. It was almost 4 am. The constant barrage of questions from detectives was, as they explained, so that they could get all the details of the horrific night as they were fresh in our minds. Although the interrogation was for our benefit, it felt like torture. These are details you want to forget and here I was being forced to remember. It felt as if someone pinned my eyelids back so they could throw as much salt in them as possible.

One haunting feature I will never forget about sitting there in the precinct was this-watching my 3 year old brother playing with a Bart Simpson figurine on a skateboard (a little fringe benefit from the McDonald's Happy Meal a detective kindly bought us). Bart Simpson kept him occupied as he drove it back and forth, back and forth. But I knew his ears were perked, listening to the questions being thrown at my sister and I. My sister couldn't stop crying. The little 8 year old looked as if she aged 30 years. Pain was scarred all over her face. I tried not to cry because I realized my siblings fed off of me. But I couldn't stop. My eyes were virtual dams drowning in tears. My head felt like it was in the middle of a nutcracker with two large men were on either side pushing against it with all their might. I just wanted to scream and never stop screaming. Years of frustration from infancy culminated in one fateful night when my father finally came through with his two decade old threat to kill my mother.

Child welfare services waited in the precinct for me and my siblings to take us to our respective orphanages. They were going to split us up because of the large age ranges. My favorite uncle, Uncle Timothy, stepped up and begged for us to be allowed to go to our grandmother's house at least for that weekend. Luckily, his request was granted, but of course, welfare agents would later have to come to inspect the home to see if we would be allowed to stay permanently.

Upon leaving the police station, the throbbing in my head just got worst. I knew there would be a crowd at my grandmother's house which was the central meeting place for the family. On a night like this, my siblings and I needed all the support and all the hugs we could get. As I suspected, there was a crowd of silent sad faces everywhere. But when Aunt Celeste, my mother's youngest sister (In her late 20's at the time) ran up to me and said, "I'm going to make you guys rich!", I was taken aback.

Rich? Even if that were so, is that something that children who just witnessed their father murder their mother and who barely got out of the house alive, want to hear? Obviously my aunt thought that money brought some sort of great, god-like comfort to the bereaved. Even though I knew Aunt Celeste had a thirst for everything expensive, from clothes to shoes to cars etc, I never thought she would be so cold.

My mom was always her 'bridge over troubled water'. Whenever she had disagreements with the other brothers and sisters (and there were many), she always ran to my mother for some solace and a shoulder to cry on. My mother was always there for her through her many failed business ideas, from T-shirt designing to her food delivery service in Park Slope. My mother always bought her goods and encouraged her. Who knows? Maybe she even helped to fund these fast-money making schemes. Whatever the case, my mom was her rock just as she was with all of her other 11 brothers and sisters, including the four by her father who resided in Barbados and England.

Little did I know that my aunt's greed was a sign of things to come. It was just a doorway into a new chapter in my little life; a chapter where greed dictated everything, including the way my family treated my brother, sister and I..

This chapter of my life is very difficult to write about because it hurts to know that the overwhelming majority of my family, people who were supposed to love us children unconditionally, people who I loved, really saw us as the perfect opportunity to make some extra cash. And why not? We didn't have any parents to protect us. (We endured many unfair situations with family members; too many to list, so I will only mention a few instances).

Funds were kept from us such as Social Security etc. Later, I found out that my grandmother allowed Aunt Celeste to claim all three of us on her tax return every single year. We never saw a cent. She continued to file for my sister and I even when I started working and filing my own tax return. Unbelievably, she continued even after I got married until one day the IRS caught up with her and she ended up paying back everything.

My grandmother would exorcise her demons on my siblings and I. She made it clear to us on a regular basis how much of a burden we were and the only reason she was keeping us was because our mother was her daughter. She and I ended up arguing on many occasions. The routine was always the same. When she had a gripe with me, she would complain to as many people as she could- all of her seven remaining children, my father's family, friends of the family, etc. If I didn't make up my bed one day, everyone would know. But then I noticed that her complaints were being blown out of proportion, even to the point where she would outright lie about me.

Once when I confronted her about missing funds for my siblings and I, she adamantly refused to give me any information. I told her that if she didn't give me any information, I would be forced to hire a lawyer to investigate. She then told everyone that I threatened to call the cops on her. It was so far-fetched that I started to get the calls back to back from my aunts and uncles, screaming at me, calling me ungrateful, etc. I was filled with fright. I realized that I could be accused of horrible things and no one would be in my corner to defend me. Not my mother, not my father, no one.

Chapter Sixteen

A SHELL

MY FAMILY DECIDED TO BURY my mother in a sprawling cemetery in Queens, New York. My grandmother sat me down on the kitchen table one morning and showed me a selection of grave plaques. Headstones were not allowed in her section of the cemetery. I can't remember what the other choices were. All I remembered was the bronze-looking one with maple leaves. The leaves seemed to grow and twist around the entire plaque – an embroidered hint of life. This appealed to me so that was my choice. My grandmother took it upon herself to order a double grave just in case. Although this was a smart financial decision, it cast an ominous shadow over me. Was I next? Was my grandmother? Then I thought,

'Really and truly, if God did not save us that night, my grandmother would be ordering a triple grave package'.

My mom's insurance money wasn't in yet, so the family pitched in to pay for the graves and the funeral. When the money did come in, everyone asked for their money back except my favorite aunt, Abigail who was the poorest of the lot, with six children. My grandmother always made a point of this. I never forgot this either. It was a testimony to her giving spirit. She was extremely close to my mom who was ten years older. I think she looked at her as a second mother. For the most part, everyone did, being that she was the oldest girl and so easy to get along with.

When my mom laughed, it was a hearty laugh. There was nothing fake about her. She would throw her head back, eyes shut and a smile as wide as the horizon. Then her head would come back down with a "Kee Kee Kee". You really had to hear it. It was infectious. I would pass by her as she enjoyed a joke on the phone and not knowing what she was laughing at, I would laugh just because her laughter and happiness was contagious. I would imitate her laugh perfectly for her and this would just make her laugh more.

To this day, my favorite auntie misses her big sister to the point that I can see the gaping whole in her soul. She is not the same person on the outside. Her exterior is a bit angrier and rougher but her heart is still huge like my mothers. My mother would give generously to those in need – to charities or just to people she came upon who needed help. My favorite auntie is the same way. These ladies would literally take the clothes off their backs if you needed them. They were very much alike except my aunt was more aggressive than my mom. I can see why she now walks around like she has lost an arm or a leg.

That dreaded day finally came – the Wake. At my grandmother's house, which was the hub of all family gatherings, a big ruckus launched when the prison that was holding my father informed my grandmother that he was granted permission to view my mom's body before anyone else made it to the funeral home. I couldn't help but flash back in time to all the occasions my dad, plain as day and serious as a heart attack would say, "I would be the one to pull the veil over your face in your coffin."

I protested but to no avail because someone already gave my father the okay. I couldn't believe how many rights this murderer had. I don't know what went through his mind as he looked down at my mom, but it wasn't fair that he was allowed the satisfaction.

I didn't want to go to the Wake. I didn't see the point of going to look at a shell. My mother was not in that coffin, it was just a shell. She was full of life and love and laughter. That thing laying in the casket was nothing but the packaging that all of her essence came wrapped in. Without her, it was nothing. So why should I go to look at this thing, I thought.

I wasn't getting dressed like everyone else at my grandmother's house. Someone asked me why I wasn't preparing to leave. When I told them I wasn't planning on going, I thought that would be the end of the story. Not by a long shot. I never thought they would force me to go but they did. I guess I should be there because to everyone else, it was my mother laying there and being the eldest child, I would have to be present.

When I got there, without exaggeration, a little over a hundred people were already in attendance, early as ever. I just felt eyes falling all over me. My natural shyness didn't come into play this day. It was overwhelmed by other stronger emotions. I sat in the last seat in the back of the funeral parlor with my sister following everything I did. This wasn't far enough from the casket though. I could still see it and this wasn't part of my plan. Then my grandmother and aunt Abigail said, "Come sit up front". I immediately protested. Already I didn't want to be there. They should have been happy that I showed up. Now they wanted me to have a front row seat?!

Aunt Abigail clenched her teeth and stared at me with this scary demanding look. Trying not to make a scene, she insisted that I get up that instant and sit up front with my grandmother. My sister and I made our way to the seats but on the way there, I was directed to view the body. Okay. This was really getting out of hand. Now I have to view the shell? It felt as if I swallowed my heart and my stomach muscles started cramping again in an effort to get rid of it. I wanted to scream, cry, throw up, pee myself, run, pass out....Everything!!!

I saw her. She looked like she was sleeping too perfectly. Her hands were folded gently, one on top of the other. Whoever styled my mom's hair did a wonderful job of hiding all of the patches that were left behind after my father pulled out stalks of hair that night. The police had Ziploc bags filled with mommy's hair. Make-up was packed on her face, like cement. Mommy would never wear so much. And the dress - a tragic configuration of white lace upon white lace. She would never wear that! This is how I was thrown back down to reality. This wasn't mommy.

I started yelling, "That's not my mommy! That's not my mommy!" I heard my voice but I couldn't snatch it back or control it. Automatically my little sister started wailing. This started a chain reaction of other people wailing my mother's name, "Heather!"

People just started coming over to comfort us. Someone, I can't remember who, told me to touch her hand as if this would comfort me. I couldn't take it anymore. I don't know how many times I said, "This is not my mommy", but before I knew it, my sister and I were escorted outside of the parlor into the lobby.

It was much brighter and airier there although many people were still bustling around. I floated around like a ghost. I can't remember any comforting words anyone tried to say to me that day. All I remember is one of my father's friends nicknamed Dutch, standing up and looking pissed when he said, "I could be home watching Jeopardy."

Could this day get any worse? If he really had to say this out loud, couldn't he have waited for me to get out of ear shot? For that moment, Dutch represented my father. I wanted to release all the anger I had onto this ½ of a man. I imagined myself beating him down to a pulp until he apologized. But instead, I backed away from him.

I ended up telling a relative when we returned home and that just caused another big ruckus at my grandmother's house. Many big ruckuses came to pass. The root cause – Everyone, with the exception of Dutch, missed mommy and they didn't know what to do with themselves. They couldn't get their hands on my father, so they just walked around angry.

I used to hear my mom say that she didn't have any friends. She said I was her best friend. I melted when she told me that not too long before she died. It was better than her telling me that she loved me, which she didn't say very often. She really didn't have to anyway. It was obvious.

The next day was the funeral. I can not remember one thing that happened at that funeral, not one word of the service, nothing. All I remember is that it took place at a church. As my sister and I, accompanied by other relatives, sat in the limo on the way to the cemetery, I couldn't help but stare at the Hearse in front of us. A shell laid inside of the coffin, not my mom. Pulling into the cemetery triggered all of my insides to turn to butterflies. My stomach started turning to painful knots again, making me want to keel over. All the while when we were driving, I was hoping we weren't going to bury my mother's body. I was hoping we were headed to an amusement park and my mother would jump out from behind some ride and yell, "Gotcha!", throwing her head back in laughter, Kee Kee Kee!

Seeing all of the graves and sad flowers lined up perfectly made me want to wiggle my nose like Samantha in Bewitched and be somewhere else. The moon would have been a good destination spot.

Everyone in the car stopped talking immediately. I hated the silence. I saw my mother's "final resting place" coming up in the distance; a freshly dug grave with dingy grave diggers standing there waiting for us to hurry up.

The road to get there was long but not long enough. My uncles helped my grandmother, who had a painfully arthritic walk, out of the limo. My sister and I followed apprehensively.

Twenty some odd cars were lined up behind us like standing dominoes. I had no idea the procession was that long. Then two Greyhound buses pulled up noisily. I recognized my mom's co-workers whom she shared many a joke with over the phone. They filed out of the bus one by one. I couldn't believe how many people were there in all. "And she said she didn't have any friends?" I said out loud really meaning to keep that thought inside.

We all made our way slowly to the gravesite. This was the worst of all. This was real. I couldn't imagine myself out of this one. I tried not to cry but I ended up bawling my head off especially when the coffin descended slowly with the help of the thick green straps on the sides. My sister followed suit but she also started vomiting all over the grass and herself. We stopped for a brief moment when my grief-stricken uncle, my mom's oldest brother, found a big rock and threw it on top of the coffin as it rested in the whole. It left a big dent. The two grave diggers looked at each other in disbelief. My mom's second oldest brother found a rock for himself too and threw it onto the coffin making a second dent. "No one is going to take my sister's coffin! No one!" He proclaimed. They both kept walking around saying the same thing in different ways. Now and then you would hear them scream my mom's name, "Heather!" That was their way of coping. I believe they thought that if they called her name long enough and loud enough, she would appear.

Chapter Seventeen

TRANSITIONING

ALTHOUGH TIMES WERE ROUGH, I felt so fortunate to be able to bypass placement in a strange temporary home by the flawed child welfare system. I thanked God for allowing my brother, sister and I to be able to stay together as a family; a broken family but a family none the less.

My grandmother's house was nice and roomy but her neighborhood was falling sharply because of a fairly new phenomenon that I call, "The Age of the Crackhead". All of a sudden the sidewalks were covered in clear crack vials with red, yellow and blue tops mixed in. When I walked to high school, not a day passed that I didn't crunch on some vials even though I tried my best to avoid them. It was much worse in front of the school. It was as if crack elves showed up in the middle of the night with sacks of empty vials and poured them all around the school grounds. Some kids turned crunching crack vials into a sport.

My grandma had an amazing green thumb. She created an oasis among the bricks of Brownsville, Brooklyn; a fertile garden in the backyard where she grew tomatoes, string beans, mint and squash. The grass was lush and over-lapping like waves in the sea. She had a beautiful rose bush in the back of the garden and its soft white blossoms blew all over my grandmother's green. It was better than a painting. The neighbors next door had a cherry tree that blew pink blossoms over as well. When they flew, they scented the air with the most perfect perfume imaginable. The owners of the tree welcomed the children in the neighborhood to pick as many cherries as they liked every spring. They grew till they were full and round and sweet, all without artificial assistance from toxic chemicals.

My grandma had potted plants in the shape of swans on the back porch and hanging on the front porch. They added more character to the house that already had it in abundance. Not too long after we moved in, she had to bring the remaining ones inside the house because crackheads would steal them during the night.

Apparently, they watched when my siblings and I moved in and took advantage of that. One night, they snuck into the front gate and broke the lock on the garage. We had a huge TV box filled with all of our toys including our dolls, the Barbie ice cream shop, cars and other Barbie play things, our bikes, my Mario Cement Factory video game, our chemistry set, a guitar and casio that I used to create theme music for the little films I made with my sister, etc. There were some toys that I kept for at least a decade and now they were all gone. It's a good thing I didn't want to part with my Mickey Mouse that I had since I was five years old. It was a gift my mother gave me when she took me to Walt Disney World in Florida to get away from my father for a minute. We stayed with my godmother and I remember her urging my mom to make a new life in Florida away from my father, but she didn't. The Mickey was tattered but I slept with it every night. I imagined hugging mommy when I hugged it in bed. Anyway, the crackheads stole everything! They did not leave a thing behind. My sister and I were beyond livid. We felt as though the whole world was out to get us.

Just a year after we moved to our grandmother's house, one morning on the way to school just about two blocks away, I noticed a disheveled looking man watching me from a distance as he walked in the same direction as me crossing Linden Boulevard. It was a challenge trying to cross the boulevard as cars and trucks sped down the six lane highway in both directions. The island platforms were so skinny that I don't think they were meant for pedestrians to stand on. Anyway, I concentrated on crossing, not the man.

Halfway down a lonely block he rushed up on me and put me in a head lock, dragging me into someone's driveway. He demanded that I give him money. I was a 17 year old with a bus pass. Trembling, I told him I didn't have any.

He then grabbed my hands and took my gold ring with my initial on it and my sister's that I borrowed that day. Our parents bought these for us from Panama. He also took my tiny gold earrings. He then proceeded to examine the plastic beaded Rastafarian necklace on me that aunt Abigail gave me. I felt so violated. He decided not to take it. I guess it was too cheap for his taste.

Then he started looking around behind him and then further back behind the driveway we were in. Something told me he was going to drag me behind there and do who knows what to me! I started screaming at the top of my lungs for God. I actually screamed, "Jehovah Help Me. Jehovah!!!"

He yelled at me with this scary voice. "Shut up!" I didn't care. I just continued to yell louder than him. "Jehovah!" Then he screamed, "If you don't shut up, I'm gonna shoot you!" I didn't see a gun on him but the mere thought of him shooting me after I escaped my own father shooting me scared the hell out of me. I shut up instantly.

At that very moment, a man pulled up in a car, staring down the driveway. My assailant walked away as cool as a cucumber, back towards Linden Boulevard. I started crying hysterically as I walked back out on to the sidewalk. The man in the car stepped out and asked me if I knew that man. I was appalled and it was apparent by the way I said, "No! He just robbed me!"

"Are you okay?" The man asked.

Seeing that I was still alive and not sexually violated, I said yes. Then the man said something that I will never forget; something that brings me comfort when I feel like I'm alone. He said, "Something told me to come back home."

This man owned the very house whose driveway the thief dragged me down. His street was a one way street spilling in from Linden Boulevard which is a huge highway that stretches for miles. A major intersection that connects Kings Highway, Remsen Avenue, Church Avenue and Linden Boulevard is right around the block. It would have taken a lot for him to go around and re-enter his street again. But he followed that voice and I am so glad he did. He offered to take me around to look for this guy but I just asked him to take me home and he did. I thanked him. Later, police officers drove me around to see if I would spot my assailant, but to no avail. After the incident, I was completely afraid to simply walk down the street in that neighborhood. I comforted myself with the thought that he was killed in some alley somewhere.

It felt like someone looked at my siblings and I and said, 'Let's take everything they have just for fun.' I had a lot of anger inside but none was directed toward God as some have the custom. I thanked God for saving my life AGAIN that day.

I thank him for everything including the hand-me-down clothes I received which replaced my own clothes after they could no longer fit me. I didn't grow out of my clothes. I lost weight rapidly, so they engulfed me. Natalie and I wasted away for months after mom died. It was as though we were terminally ill patients on our last leg.

Everything my 8 year old sister ate, she vomited. I apologize for the grittiness but my experience is real and this is the best way that I can express myself. Everything I ate came out as diarrhea everyday. I was naturally thin but at this point, I was unhealthy looking. In high school, my new nickname was "Stick". More important than looks, all three of us really were unhealthy.

We developed anemia. This made us more susceptible to diseases that normal immune systems would fight off. I started developing allergies to airborne allergens which culminated into me becoming an asthmatic. Every year to this day, it seems to get worst and now I'm dependent on medication that I must take every day. The stress of losing both our parents the way we did so suddenly was too much for our bodies to handle. I basically wanted to die and I continued to entertain the thought of committing suicide a lot.

Therapy was one of the best things our grandmother supplied for us. Each of us had our own therapists and it really made a difference for our psychological well being. The therapists never had to deal with children orphaned by domestic violence before so we were a good study for them. More than that, we began to feel that they genuinely cared for us. They walked us through, among other things, the court process.

A preliminary hearing was set by the District Attorney's office to determine if the case was serious enough to go to trial. Of course the case was serious enough for prosecution. This process was mandatory. The D.A. and the court appointed child psychologist (not to be confused with the ones I just mentioned) prepped me for the questions that I would be asked as I was on the stand. I remember walking into a drearily lit court room through a side door. I guess that was the door under aged witnesses entered from. Forty-some-odd faces looked annoyed at having to trek to court for jury duty. They stared at me as I climbed up the steps to the chair next to the judge. I was basically swimming in a black sweater with burgundy roses printed all over it. It was more like a sweater dress as it easily reached my knobby knees through my jeans. Over and over again, I kept pulling it up at the neck, adjusting it to not fall over my shoulder.

Although I was prepared, I was terrified. I was asked questions about the happenings of that night many times in front of a few people at a time but never a whole room of almost 50 people. The questions started okay.

"What is your name?"

I answered, "Nicole Richards. *'Good. One question out of the way.'* I thought.

"How old are you?"

"Fifteen."

'Two questions.' The easy questions kept coming until the D.A. requested,

"Please tell the court what happened on November 22nd..."

I started recapping the events from the daytime until the night, trying my best to robotically hold in my emotions. It didn't work. It was even a surprise to me when I broke down, crying hysterically. When I spoke of that night, I felt as though my body was transported there again, reliving the horror. The one person who would have been able to comfort me at this time was dead.

The D.A. asked the judge to allow me to have a moment off the stand to regroup. He granted the request and I was escorted out of the court for about 10-15 minutes. The D.A. and psychologist tried to calm me down but I calmed down on my own and in my own time. They promised that I would only be asked one more question. I agreed to enter the courtroom again. I was not expecting what I was about to witness. The entire room of once annoyed faces was now filled with faces streaming with tears. Eyes reddened and noses were being blown into tissues. I did a double take at everyone as I approached the stand again. I knew that my story was sad but I didn't know it would evoke so much sadness from strangers.

The last question the D.A. asked me was, "What is today's date?"

I answered quickly so that I could hurry up and get out of that chair. I was one week away from my 16th birthday. This is a time when an adolescent is beginning her transition into young adulthood. Here I was, wishing for my life to be over. I felt like an 80 year old who lived a long and hard life. My thoughts and my memories weighed heavily upon me. I felt old and weak and sickly depressed all the time. This was my transition into a new life; one without parents or anyone who truly loved me or my siblings; one where I was looked upon as unprotected prey to take advantage of; one where I (with the exception of my siblings) existed alone.

Chapter Eighteen

ALL THAT GLITTERS

I BELIEVE IN GOD. YOU PROBABLY noticed all my references to God so that's a given. But I wasn't always a believer so to speak. I was raised an atheist by my father. He always told me that god didn't exist and the concept of god was created to keep men under control. "I am god and you are god", he would say. He taught me that the Earth wasn't created but that it came about by chance. I believed all of his philosophy until I was ten. My parents had just finished shopping at "Big R", a large supermarket, and my mom and I waited on the platform for my father to pull up the car. I looked up at the sky which was a vibrant, aqua-type blue and the full white clouds that floated gently over the blue. It was an ethereal dance. I watched in admiration at this process that is taken for granted by us humans and said to myself, 'There must be a god'. How could something as amazing and perfect as our atmosphere come about by chance? How could the Earth, so perfect to human life, come about by chance? How could I, so precise in my design come about by chance? From that day on, I believed in God.

I loved to read and I wanted to know what was inside of the much talked about Bible which was said to be from God. My mom bought me a huge brown leathered children's Bible with illustrations galore. I loved this book. As I mentioned before, my father saw me delving into it one Saturday and forbid me from reading it again. "If I see you reading this again, I will throw it through the window!" He was a man who carried out his threats so I would hide on the far side of my bedroom underneath the bed by the light of the sun through the window. It sounds like a passage from "Flowers in the Attic", but it's true. Both my sister and I would read together.

One Sunday a man and a woman came to our door bringing 'good news' about God's kingdom. They belonged to a Christian sect. I was shocked when my father invited them in. I sat down with my father not knowing where this would go. They spoke a little about Jesus' teachings and explained how he was sent to Earth to proclaim God's coming kingdom in the future. To my surprise my father asked questions but I soon found out he was only setting them up to try to catch them in some intellectual trap. He went on to argue with them for over an hour. Debating, arguing really, was one of his past times. He laughed at them, a condescending laugh and tried his darndest to make them look and feel stupid. But the couple continued on the defense, armed with their Bibles and memorized scriptures; they flipped the pages with lightening speed- an onslaught of bullets aimed at my father and his empty reasonings. Then, as time ran away, they started looking at their watches and excused themselves as their other 'friends' must be looking for them. They left a book with me called, *Bible Stories for Children* and highlighted a vibrant illustration from the first chapter with Adam and Even and a whole host of animals co-existing. They left me with the thought that I could live forever in a paradise on Earth just like the paradise called Eden that God intended for all humans.

Two years later, when Natalie, Nash and I were officially placed with our maternal grandmother, she had just started studying the Bible with members of this same religion. The main 'man of the cloth' in this church and his wife, studied with my grandmother and her sister. I will call them Brother and Sister T.

Brother and Sister T had an 'adopted daughter' (I will go into depth later) who was 9 years older than me. They assigned her to study the Bible with Natalie and me. Their wide smiles and overly happy dispositions gave me the creeps at first. Then they gave my sister and I hope; the hope that we would see our mother again in a Paradise on Earth in the near future. They played to the need that my sister and I longed for. Our mother was just killed a couple weeks earlier and this really was 'good news' indeed! From this point on, I was hooked. The teachings of this religion, which were spoon fed to me everyday, really seemed to fill that fresh gaping whole in my soul. Everything seemed to glitter, until my eyes started to open...steadily.

Chapter Nineteen

RELIGION IS LIKE CANDY

RELIGION IS LIKE CANDY. THE way that it's wrapped determines who will eat it. If I like shiny silver wrappings, I will go after the candy wrapped in silver. If you prefer the simple waxy wrappings, you will grab that. But then there are some people who are like children in that they'll simply eat anything as long as it's sweet.

Presentation is everything and the reason why I bring this up is because the religion in question here (which they say is not "a" religion but the "The Truth") was presented to my sister and I in the most appealing wrapping we had ever seen. It promised that we would see our mother in a paradise on Earth. What could be sweeter than that?!

She would be resurrected from her sleep when God awakens all those in their memorial tombs. Now this may very well be so, but the fine print was the key. The only way we would be able to see her is if we became part of and followed along the lines of this religion - God's only true organization on Earth, with its many rules and regulations. We were taught and believed that the rules and regulations really weren't burdensome at all but were for our benefit, protecting us from Satan's world and the harm that it would exact upon us, being that we, as God's only true followers on Earth, were Satan's primary targets.

All my little sister and I cared about was seeing our mother again and at that point, we would do whatever it took to do so. Thus, we started our Bible studies.

I will be speaking about my experience with this religion because it played a major role in my life as I lived as a baptized member for 12 years.

It is important that people in abusive relationships with children and the abuser see how unprotected and opened to the world and its many vices their children will be if they died or if they are imprisoned for the murder of their significant other. I am just sharing my experience as a girl who was orphaned when my father killed my mother after years of abuse. I was very much an open field to the world and most of the confusion I endured was at the hands of my extended family and members of this religion.

Sister T, the wife of the main pastor who studied the Bible with my grandmother, was a very stern woman who walked painfully upright and looked as if she was in anguish every time she smiled. Smiling and looking happy is a must for all members because to the world, they should always appear be the happiest people on Earth since they are, in their words, God's chosen people. Also, "worldly people" should be attracted to this religion when noticing how sterling and jovial they are in comparison to the rest of the ailing world.

Anyway, I wanted to share one of my latest poems with Sister T. I was very shy as a child and didn't share my poems with everyone. Sharing one of my poems with someone was sharing a piece of me - a piece of my soul. The poem is entitled, *Valley of My Eye*. It was born out of the utter sadness I felt losing my mother and the continuous struggle to stay afloat without her.

Valley of My Eye

I took a trip, up a mountain, the highest
Steep was its full mass
Dents, chasms the wretched I topped
I bathed in glory at last

But behold an abyss, depth and width
As spacious as the sky
Where solid fog stayed still and slept
Valley of my eye

Grassy green half staffed and stunted
Grief's whirlwind now loom
But look I saw another pang
Black roses in full bloom

Weeping willows stood their ground
Robins lost their soft song
Salty streams of tears came forth
Why do they flow so long?

And then a tremor shook the earth
A godly sight to see
My traveling companion, my steps of fear
My mountain majesty

I must climb again, this thing the highest
Echoing one steep cry
To come upon it again, I dread
Valley of my eye

When I finished reading, Sister T began to laugh. And the laughter got louder and more condescending. She then said, "Mountain majesty?", and started laughing again. My heart sank as I looked at her. I was already in the process of indoctrination so I automatically thought, 'What did I do wrong?" She told me that only God can have the title of Majesty and then she proceeded to go into her Bible to show me scriptures to back this up.

This became a routine that I would be subjected to on a regular basis; having the Bible used as a tool to whip me into shape. Sister T also saw a short story I was writing for school which was set in Ancient Egypt and involved Pharaoh's and mummies and Egyptian gods. She told me this was an absolute no-no.

"A true worshipper of God can not entertain or be involved in idolatry and essentially false religion." She said as she pulled out the Bible and in seconds, found the scriptures to back up her statement. I wanted to do what was right at all times and fit into the religion, (it hurts to even write this) so I severed ties with my best friend that I had since I was 6 years of age. My friend who stuck with me and carried me through the most difficult times of my life – Writing. As I mentioned earlier, writing was my defense mechanism. It was very valuable to me, but if I wanted to see my mother again in the near future, I had to align myself with God's "one true religion". From that point, I didn't write as a hobby for ten years straight.

The place of worship that we attended seemed to be divided in terms of Americans vs. Caribbean people. This was in the words of some of the members. According to Brother T, the American pastors were jealous of his position as the main pastor and they would do anything to have him ousted. Gossip stirred that he was helping illegal immigrants to gain temporary legal status through a Green card scam.

One day, an American elder who never spoke to me for the year I was attending the congregation finally decided to ask to accompany me as a partner as everyone preached the word from door to door one Saturday morning. After the regular greetings, he went straight to the jugular and asked me,

"So…Did Brother T help you get your green card?"

I honestly didn't know what a green card was back then.

"A Green Card?" I asked.

He must have realized that he overstepped his boundaries because he then asked me,

"Are you American?"

With that I responded, "Yes."

He apologized and then walked away to go from door to door by himself. I had to partner up with two other members for the rest of the morning. I didn't mind because he made me feel very uncomfortable.

I mentioned this to Brother and Sister T and that was when they told me about the whole supposed scheme to have him step down. Brother T went on to tell me, Natalie and other young ones they were studying the Bible with that we were the pillars of the congregation and it could not stand without us. So we had to be very careful not to give people any information about us or else they'll try to destroy us. This kind of paranoia talk was surprising and weird but all of us young ones obeyed. Every time we attended the five weekly religious meetings, we would have to watch our back and watch our tongue. At the beginning, most people avoided me because I communicated with Brother and Sister T and their 'adopted daughter'.

There was a lot more divisive talk coming from Brother T that I never mentioned to my guardian. At the time, Brother and Sister T were really good to us, taking us on excursions and inviting us to dinner and my guardian put a lot of faith in them. They spoke a lot of hateful things about my guardian too, calling her a greedy old woman etc., but I never let her know. This would have shaken her spiritual foundation.   I never knew if the Green Card scandal was true but I did find out that something even more sinister was happening under the roof of Brother and Sister T's home, which coincidentally, was right over the church.

I mentioned earlier that they 'adopted' the young lady who studied the Bible with me (I will call her Tanya). She came from an abusive home in the Caribbean. Her father sexually abused her and her mother, knowing this, physically abused her. Brother and Sister T rescued her and brought her to the U.S. Not too long after I was baptized, she confided in me. Apparently Brother T continued in her father's footsteps and sexually abused her for the whole time she was living with the couple. She told me how big his penis was, identifying marks on it and how often he would come to her bedroom. She felt that she couldn't say anything since she was illegal in the U.S. and she didn't have anywhere else to go. I told her that my grandmother would be more than happy to take her in but she reminded me that would be a conflict since she was so close to the couple.

Tanya talked me into helping her get an apartment since I was an American citizen. It was right around the corner from my grandmother's house. That's when I moved out to help Tanya with the rent and also to get away from my family's verbal abuse and false accusations. But right before she left Brother and Sister T's apartment she reported Brother T's abuses to the pastors in the congregation. The pastors spoke to him and of course, he denied everything.

I was asked to sit before three pastors and recount everything Tanya told me concerning Brother T. I felt like I was in court again. I was told by the body of pastors that I could not discuss this matter with anyone outside of the little room in the basement of the church and I obeyed.

The end result was that Brother T was never disciplined since, according to him, indiscretions never took place and the pastors didn't have enough evidence to prove that anything ever did occur. But the decision concerning Tanya never made sense.

She was disciplined for allowing Brother T to have sex with her. So essentially, the pastors saw this as fornication as opposed to what it really was, molestation. And how can someone be disciplined for fornication if according to the other undisciplined party, it never occurred? Tanya's privileges of preaching from door to door and answering questions at the services (which she thrived off of) were taken away from her.

Interestingly enough, a fornicator is usually ousted from the church. They can come to the services but no one is allowed to speak with them for a certain period of time determined by the pastors. It is as if they do not exist. It could take weeks, months or even years for the "sinner's" privileges to be restored. But in Tanya's case, if she received that discipline, everyone in the congregation would question why the other party, Brother T didn't receive the same. Everything was kept hush-hush but, of course, with time, the rumor mill started to churn.

People turned up a smug nose at Tanya and even to me sometimes for being in her company.

One day Tanya wanted to prove a point to me. She told me to tell Brother T that I didn't mean to speak against him to the other pastors and to convince him that I believed him over her. I did that one day on my grandmother's porch. He seemed elated. He took my hand into his and said to me with a big, dirty smile on his face, "You and I will become really good friends." I felt icky.

Somehow, she already knew that he would respond that way toward me. She said, "You see. He would replace me with you." Did I really need to have to go through that? In her mind, I guess I did.

I believe that what she said occurred but I realized after some time that Tanya herself was a desperate, wounded soul because she started developing a jealousy toward me. I was American, I was younger than her and I was virgin. That was enough for her to hate me. To make a long story short, she insulted me every chance she got. She was critical of everything I did, including the way I drank juice. She made me feel indebted to her for bringing "The Truth" to me so I basically became her servant, running out all hours of the night to buy her food etc. She ended up telling whoever would listen that I, a virgin who had never been kissed, was having sex with the gang members in our apartment building. When her brother, a little older than me, tried to come on to me, she treated me similar to how the pastors and I suspect her mom treated her -Like I was a slut. This was the last straw that forced me to move out of that apartment and back with my grandmother.

I have experienced many other mind boggling events being a part of this religion including surviving an attempted solicitation by a seventy-something year old man who held a high position. His way to get close to me was by telling me, "Since you don't have a father, I want to be a father to you. And since you are at the age where you will be getting married soon, (age 20) I don't want you to be afraid when you see a penis for the first time, so I'm going to show you mine."

I excused myself and rushed out of his office with my virginity and dignity still intact but everything else broken. Years later I got up enough nerve to report it to the pastors in a new congregation that I joined but in the end, I was disciplined. The other party, of course, was not. Talk about a record on repeat. I had enough.

My original congregation has since been dissolved. In effect, it no longer exists and the members ended up being absorbed into neighboring congregations. Although I saw a lot of hypocrisy and madness that I should not have been privy to, there are valuable things that I took from my experience as a member of this religion - Great friendships and more importantly, a good overall knowledge of Bible scriptures whereas before I had none. I believe God allows us to experience situations for a certain amount of time for a reason. If the reason is not apparent at the moment, it becomes apparent later on down the line. I have since left "the truth" but I continue to stay with my God.

Chapter Twenty

OPEN SEASON

THERE'S NO LOVE LIKE A mother's love. This adage may be old but it is so true. When my mother was murdered, somehow it became open season on Natalie, Nash and I. We became a forum that relatives and others could exorcise their demons. I've never seen anything like it. I came to realize that when people know that you have no parents, they look upon you like you are a piece of nothing. I learned first hand so many important aspects of human nature, from a child's perspective, that some people never learn or care to learn about in their lives.

For example, people for the most part have different faces. They have a face for work, a face for friends (depending on the friend) and a face for family. For some, the only time their real face is revealed is when they have to look in the mirror and that's only when they are not lying to themselves. For others, they reveal that true face to kids like me who they couldn't give a damn about because they had no one to answer to. As far as they were concerned, I had no protection. But little did they know that I had the highest form of protection; God's love.

When we became Wards of the Court, I was so thankful when my maternal grandmother won custody of us. After a whole night of interrogation in the police precinct, Child Protective Services waited to take the three of us into separate orphanages because we were so apart in age. One of my uncles stepped up though and begged for us to at least spend the night by my grandmother's house. Fortunately for us, we never saw the inside of an orphanage as the Administration for Children's Services (ACS), after examining my grandmother's house agreed for us to live there. I thank God for this. On the downside, when we made our entrance into my grandmother's house about 3am the next morning after leaving the police precinct, people were plastered everywhere in silent awe just staring at us. As I mentioned earlier, I was greeted with a hug from Aunt Celeste with the quote, "**I'm going to make you guys rich**." Very comforting words indeed especially when your father just shot your mother to death in your presence.

At any rate, my father has four sisters who are successful according to the world's standards. One is a doctor and the other three have their own businesses. I have five adult cousins, older than me from that brood and a grandmother. When my mother was alive, they didn't have much contact with me or my siblings. When mom died, it got worse. They supplied my father with a lawyer and didn't have any contact with us for years.

Recently, I missed a telephone call from one of those aunts on my father's side of the family. So I listened to the voice mail and she said, "Hi. I wasn't sure if this is still your number, but I tried calling your grandmother and she wasn't available so I called you." (Well of course I felt special…Not) "I am in California. If you want to call me back, here is my number ----------." When I got the message, I called her back 2 days later and when it went to voice mail, I left her a message confirming that she did call the right number and she could return my call whenever she liked. Of course she never returned my call. I think in her mind, she already did her part. The way my father's family looked down on my siblings and me used to make me feel very low. Now, I don't care as much but I must admit there is that tinge of pain I would feel for anyone rejected by their own family; anyone enduring little pity calls and pity hand outs now and then from a group of people who share the same blood as you but believe themselves to be better than you. I actually pity people like that. Thus, one of the lessons I learned was-**sometimes water is thicker than blood**.

Anyway, my mom always taught me to never ask anyone for money. She pounded this lesson of self-sufficiency and independence into my head a thousand times over. When she died, I ended up in a position where I needed immediate financial help for school. I was an honors student throughout my entire educational career. When I started college, less than two years after mom died, I still wanted to keep that record shining. My new family circumstance was one that caused the Financial Aid Office and the FAFSA a while to understand. Every time I applied for aid, I would have to provide 50 million documents including my mother's death certificate. This was heart-wrenching every year that I had to do this and even when I provided everything, it took forever for Financial Aid to understand the urgency of the situation.

So although I was able to take classes for my first year of school, I didn't have money to buy books. I asked my grandmother and other relatives on my mother's side of the family for help but all I received were rejections. So I bit a huge bullet and out of sheer desperation, I got in contact with one of my father's sisters who is a doctor. I thought for sure she would understand my situation and want to help me.

Boy was I wrong! I have never been so screamed at and accused of atrocities in my entire life! She accused me of being a thief, trying to steal her money. She called me a liar. She said that when she was going to school she didn't have to pay for books therefore I was lying for sure about needing money for books (mind you, she went to college in the 1960's or 1970's). After a couple minutes of ranting and raving she hung up the phone on me. That was my first and last conversation with my dear aunt. A year later, out of the blue, one of her sisters sent a non-refundable plane ticket for me to spend the summer with them in California. I turned it down immediately when my maternal grandmother tried to hand it to me. I saw it as a pity hand out. When my grandmother emphasized that it was non-refundable. It didn't make a difference to me. My little sister took the ticket instead. She regretted doing so afterwards though (another story).

I got through my first year of school relying on notes from professors and photo copies of chapters from fellow students. By my second year in college at age 18, I was able, after much job searching without experience, to secure a job to support my schooling habit as a teacher's assistant at a Day Care Center. The fifty dollars a week that I received off the books was not much but it was better than nothing and I thanked God for it. For the several months that I was at this job, I continued to search for a better opportunity. Nothing seemed available for me.

Times became desperate, especially when I moved out of my grandmother's house at age 19 (will expound later). I needed to pitch in with my roommate to help pay for the rent and my meager wages were not cutting it. I made a big decision to follow a shaky path. If my family found out about it, I would be looked down upon with disgrace. It was something shameful that I had to keep a secret. I saw the need to go on welfare. My roommate suggested this. At first, I would not even consider it. Then, as times got rougher for me financially, and my grades started plummeting because I couldn't afford the text books, I changed my mind. I was even kicked out of college because of poor grades. Luckily, I entered a program, "The New Start Program", which allowed me to continue my schooling in a community college while I attempted to increase my GPA.

I wanted to make sure that I made a "New Start" in the fullest sense, where I would actually have money to pay for textbooks. This was the main reason why I went on welfare. Welfare is for people in dire need and at this moment, I saw myself as such. My intention was for this to be a temporary appointment and all the while, I would continue to look for a real job. I was approved after many document-ladened trips to the welfare offices in downtown Brooklyn.

A fairly new program was in the works back then called, "The Work Experience Program" (WEP). I would be employed by a State agency in exchange for food stamps and a $260.00 check that would go towards my monthly rent. That was fine for me because now, I could actually put some work experience on my blank resume. Fortunately, before I actually was assigned to a work place, I had to attend several orientation classes which taught me how to compose my own resume, how to carry myself in a job interview and all the other tools I needed to get and keep a job.

I had a choice of either working as an administrative assistant or doing manual labor, such as janitorial work. I chose administrative duties but because I was enrolled in college as a day student, I was told there were no administrative positions available in the evening. I had to take what was given me. Like I said before, it was better than nothing.

I started working immediately at the Health Building on Worth Street in Manhattan. I had to report to a supervisor; a tall, lanky looking chimney sweep of a man who seemed to be a recovering addict of some sort. He towered over me like an old tree that saw one too many winter storms and when he spoke, it was as if years of built up cigarette smoke was finally released.

"You're assigned to clean all of the bathrooms, Men and Women's, on the 4th and 5th floors."

He seemed a bit too happy to relay that information to me.

I made my way upstairs with a partner who would show me the ropes of bathroom cleaning. I was mortified at first but happy that my lot wasn't as bad as it was a few weeks before. It was lonely at night although there were several workers like myself bustling around. Whenever I had a break, I would go down to the basement in the dingy locker room and study. In retrospect, I see how unsafe it was for me to be down there in that lonely space at night. If anyone wanted to attack me, my screams would not have been heard. Sometimes I would stay at this job until 12 midnight. I would always find myself falling asleep on the train on the way home. I discovered the ability to stand and sleep at the same time.

A few months into my appointment on Worth Street, an information Kiosk was placed in the main lobby of the Health Building. I few of us would press its buttons haphazardly out of sheer boredom in between tasks. I was polishing the walls and doors of the main elevators when it caught my eye. I went over to check it out and Mayor Giuliani's smiling face greeted me on the screen. There was a prompt for suggestions for the mayor. Gullible me thought that the mayor would actually read suggestions from little people like me. I wrote about my experience growing up with my parents and I suggested that children orphaned by domestic violence and other orphans who are trying to improve their lives by going to college really shouldn't be subjected to cleaning duties as part of the WEP Program.

My plea for help on Mayor Giuliani's Kiosk became my nightly ritual. After many nights of the mayor's smiling face and my feverish typing without a response, I started to finally get the real picture. This was not the forum for me to get the mayor's attention but it became a way for me to vent my frustration.

Sometimes I would work in the daytime if I didn't have classes. Working in the day had its pros and cons. I would actually get some time set aside at night to sleep but then, I was subjected to the endless flow of employees and visitors to the Health Building. I tried to hide my face from people as I swept the floors with a big industrial broom that was literally bigger than me. The mop and the bright yellow bucket that I had to drag behind me didn't help my attempts to conceal myself.

There were a group of teenagers around my age who worked in the building part time in a program they were placed in by their parents who were full time employees. They always traveled in a pack, like wildebeests. There were about 9 of them - seven girls and two boys. Every time I would see them, I would try to turn the corner or put my head down. These were my peers so it would have been more than shameful for them, somewhat privileged kids, to see me, a lowly girl, throwing out trash or pushing a broom.

Well that fateful day came. They must have been on their way to hunt for lunch or something when they spotted me, pushing this heavy mop around the lobby. I was almost done with what felt like a struggle to make the floors shine. Although my bright yellow signs that read, "Caution – Wet Floor" were placed all over, they took it upon themselves to walk right through the middle of the wet floors. My humiliation and anger intermingled. I stood up straight to see them, some with their noses up in the air, some staring at me dead in the face, all of them laughing hysterically. I wanted someone, anyone to slip and fall but some wishes don't come true.

The anger that I felt heightened so much so that after that moment, it overshadowed the embarrassment. I still felt humiliated but I resolved after that day to stop hiding and to stand with my head held high, even if I had a mop in my hand.

When I would clean offices, throwing their garbage out, I would speak to everyone in a friendly manner whereas before shame made me fold under myself, hiding who I truly was inside-a happy go lucky sometimes comical creature. Soon, almost everyone in the building knew me or knew of me. A day wouldn't pass without me smiling or trying to tell some joke. This was my temporary lot and I was going to make the most of it. Many of the employees of the Health Building tried to put in a good word for me to get a real job but the outcome was always the same - I didn't have enough experience.

Apparently, my chimney sweep of a supervisor didn't like my new found happiness. In his broken language, he would heckle me while I cleaned.

"Look at cha. You can't even sweep good. Walkin' roun' here like you Naomi Campbell or somethin'."

At that, I would push the broom and pretend to walk down a catwalk for the whole length of the lobby floor, to one end and back again. This enraged him. He would go outside to take a smoke and then return again, just to stare at me to unnerve. This went on for weeks until one evening when I had to get a key for a custodial closet from him. I went to his office and saw a young woman around my age sitting down, just hanging out and laughing with the supervisor. This young woman, who came in after me, somehow got an evening administrative job. 'Hmmmm', I thought.

The supervisor looked as if he was high on something. He came at me with the key, dangling it in front of my face.

"You know you don't have to be cleanin' dis place. You could work up here with me in da office."

"Really?" I asked sarcastically, not at all interested.

"Yeah. You know what you gotta do."

"Ask someone in the central office?" I asked knowing full well what he meant.

The young woman started laughing but he was as serious as can be. I just took the key and made my way out as fast as I could. I told my cleaning partner that night what happened in the office. Next thing I knew, two male workers approached me with a scheme. News really flies fast. They wanted me to report the supervisor for sexual harassment, adding that he attempted to rape me, so that I could sue New York State and they could act as witnesses, thus getting some of the money I would win. I guess they saw this as their way out. I immediately declined but they continued to try to talk me into their dishonest proposal.

The very next day, I was called to some board of supervisors of the WEP Program. My supervisor was apparently very upset that I didn't fall for his advances. He claimed that I was a poor worker, just goofing off without any respect for authority. He also claimed that I was always late or just missing when he needed me to clean. The board kicked me out of the program solely on this man's claims but I filed for an appeal.

I made an appointment and pled my case to a room full of suited men and women. I felt as though my life was just full of court cases one after the other. A flood of frustration welled forth and I told them my whole story in a nutshell. I just wanted to make a life for myself, minding my own business, going to school and trying to do everything right. When I was done, everyone resembled the jury in my father's preliminary trial but they were better at holding back tears. In the end, the tall, lanky, chimney sweep of a man was demoted. He was much quieter from that day on.

This did not bring me joy. I felt a growing urgency. I knew I had to push even harder to get myself out of this WEP program. At school I inquired about the Work Study program. It is a program designed to help students in financial need. If there was an opening for me and if I was qualified, I would work for wages in a department in the school during the day whenever I wasn't in class. I applied for this program before but never received a response until now. This was heaven sent. I went in for an interview in the "College Now" program in a pleasant office using the skills I learned in the orientation classes for WEP, and aced it.

After almost a year, I could finally walk out of WEP and welfare and without the help of the brainless Kiosk. Although the shame was great when I began the program,

I learned how to stand up and be proud of myself even if everyone around me tried to make me feel small. I learned how to open my mouth and defend myself. I also learned some good cleaning tips that I still keep with me to this day. This was just a part of my Wilderness before the Promised Land.

Chapter Twenty One

THE AGE OF SAGITTARIUS

I WAS ALWAYS A SHY GIRL growing up. I had a lot to say but I never found my voice beyond paper. I was always afraid to speak up and speak out. I kept quiet when my father would beat my mother and this quiet demeanor transcended throughout every facet of my life.

My mother was not deep into astrology by any means but she entertained herself with it now and again. She had a little wooden plaque that was an Ode to Sagittarius hung in a corner of our basement. She and I shared this unique sign. The plaque listed the attributes of the Sagittarian but there was one word that I wasn't familiar with – candid. I quickly grabbed my children's dictionary and looked it up as I always would when I came across a word I didn't know. When I read the meaning: frank, blunt, outspoken,

I said to myself, 'This is not me.' So like any inquisitive 10 year old child, I asked my mother, "How come the plaque says Sagittarians are supposed to be candid and I'm not?" My mother smiled at me and said, as you get older, you will grow into your Sagittarian self. So from that moment I looked forward to being more outspoken, blunt, frank, and candid. It would take a few years after my mom died before I found a voice and started to 'grow into my Sagittarian self'. This transition came about as a result of being pushed to the limit though.

Living with my grandmother was a blessing and disaster. I was so very grateful that Natalie, Nash and I were not put in foster care and we were able to stay together as a family. But on the other side, my grandmother's house was where my siblings and I learned what full on adversity felt like. My grandmother was 64 years old and living in her four bedroom home with her husband and some relatives who were tenants in the basement. I guess all the space prompted the Child Welfare Services to back off and the State of New York to award her legal guardian status.

I was very grateful for my grandmother, after all, she took us in even when my father's family, with the exception of one, wanted nothing to do with us. I was very grateful, so much so, I stomached a lot of the ill treatment.

My sister, brother and I were like pets left in a will by a deceased owner to people who were allergic to us. I say people because my mother's two sisters and five brothers were in our lives just as much as our grandmother was. We really tried to be as quiet, helpful and out of sight as children who have just lost their mother to the hands of their father could be, but that was not good enough. Our grandmother always found something about us to complain about. When she would complain, it would revolve around my sister and I not helping her out with house work. When we would try to pick up a broom or a mop, we would get the same comments; "Put that down. You don't know what you're doing." Or "I just cleaned that, what are you doing?" I think my grandmother just needed something to complain about. She needed attention because raising three children after you have already raised eight on your own and at age 64 was no easy feat. As much as we tried to be out of the way, she needed some kind of emotional support and I believe she thought by complaining about us to everyone gave her the support she thought she needed.

We were like her sounding board and why not, her child, her first daughter was murdered by our father and we were always a constant reminder of that. Worst yet, my little sister resembled my father and she would always be reminded of how much she looked like him and acted like him. I was very close to my father growing up so my grandmother would always tell me how I loved my father more than I loved my mother. She even told me that I was the reason why my mother died because instead of calling the police that night, I called her. I blamed myself for my mom's death for years to come because of my grandmother's statements.

My grandmother's husband or my step-grandfather, when he wasn't taking his daily walk to the local OTB, he spent most of his time sitting in front of a tiny black and white television in one corner of the kitchen, watching us and sucking his teeth at us every time we passed by. He would throw his little discouraging comments at us now and then.

Once I tried my inexperienced hand at cooking and my step-grandfather got up from his chair that imprinted his gluteus maximus and slid his slippered feet towards me as if to throw something in the garbage just so he could see what I was doing. He looked into my boiling pot, looked at me and laughed this condescending laugh. I asked him what was wrong. He told me smiling, "You don't know what you're doing. Why don't you get out of the kitchen?"

This is how it was on a regular basis but everyday was worse than the one before. I used to privately call my grandmother the first World-wide web or the prototype to the World-wide web because no one could contact as many people in so short a time as my grandmother's speedy fingers would as she dialed numbers when she had a piece of juicy gossip. Her complaints reached the far ends of the earth. Then Natalie and I, being the oldest ones, would hear about it from our aunts and uncles and elders from the church. The aunts and uncles would come on the phone without question, yelling at me. They seemed to be the Borg from Star Trek as they all had the same things to say in order -"Why are you treating my mother like this?! You guys are so ungrateful! You could be living on the streets if it wasn't for my mother…!'"

I would stay quiet as they spewed their regular spiel. Natalie, on the other hand, was always outspoken. From the beginning when we would be attacked, she would be ready for war, equaling and surpassing their boisterousness with her loud voice. She seemed to have no fear and she was my sibling by 8 years. I always admired this fearlessness about her. Gratefully, her strong personality has never waned.

The calls would usually come back to back and I would usually sit there quietly listening, guilty for just existing. Then one day at the age of 17 I couldn't take it anymore. My grandmother called me to the phone in the kitchen where she and her husband sat at either end of the table to speak to one of my uncles. She had this accomplished smile on her face as usual and my step-grandfather was one second away from pulling out his virtual popcorn for the show. Of course I knew what kind of call this was. I took the rotary phone receiver from her and before I could say 'hello' properly, the yelling and the accusations started flying towards me. I surprised myself when I raised my voice slightly but authoritatively and said,

"I'm seventeen years old. I'm not a child anymore. When you can learn to respect me and lower your voice when speaking to me, then we can talk. Other than that, this conversation is over!"

Then I hung up the rotary phone and walked away. My audience was dumbfounded. They were fortunate enough to witness the moment I grew into my Sagittarian self. It felt good to stand up for myself but I still had a lot to learn and a lot of growth to experience.

Chapter Twenty Two

ENTER THE DRAGON...LADY

SEVENTEEN WAS A GOAL AGE for me since I was ten. I vowed to myself that I would be a successful child writing prodigy by the age of seventeen. I saw myself sitting in front of Matt Lauer, being interviewed about my latest book. This is why I wrote so many poems and stories until my mother died when I was fifteen. Although my circumstances changed drastically, seventeen became the age I made a resolve not to be anyone's punching bag anymore.

My grandmother continued my mother's overprotective ways so I was hardly outside of the house. Looking back now I can understand her concern. Natalie, Nash and I were the only pieces of her daughter that existed and she wanted to keep these pieces in tact.

Anyway, I was seventeen living in New York City and I hadn't even ridden the train by myself. I made up my mind to get on the train for the first time alone. My destination? Newark, New Jersey, where a family that belonged to the church lived. When I told my grandmother, she had a conniption. She stood by the kitchen door that led to the backyard and started yelling at me, asking me if I was crazy. I told her that I was going to see my friends regardless if she liked it or not.

My step-grandfather, as he sat in his sad memory foam, egged her on. Then, as I can remember clear as day, my grandmother screamed, "Then I hope a train runs over you!" I can't say that I couldn't believe what my ears were hearing. The words just made no sense. They cut me but not deep enough to stop me from venturing beyond the house. I wanted to travel to Newark even more so. I told her that was a very horrible thing to say and then I left.

Reading subway maps and signs, I learned, is not difficult. On the train ride I thought about my grandmother's remark, "I hope a train runs over you", and I wallowed in the pain that I felt. Losing my parents and being criticized and called names by the people who were supposed to love me, hurt me so much. The emotional pain became physical pain. This is how you know you are being subjected to too much. When the emotional pain passes that threshold and grips your bones and joints and affects your breathing. Stress is a hell of a thing.

I wallowed so much in my own pain as an adolescent that I forgot the pain that my grandmother must have been going through. Her doctor prescribed sleeping pills because she couldn't sleep at night on her own since her first daughter was killed. As I look back, I realize that she blamed me for her daughter's death because my father wasn't there for her to vent her anger to. She picked at me and criticized me a lot because she was in pain and needed someone to transfer that pain to. I don't think my grandmother meant any harm. She was just caught up in the un-naturalness of it all. She was also from the old school which was a bit rougher so even before my mom died, when my grandmother would baby sit me as a young child, I could feel the love from her beyond the abrasiveness. I think she couldn't believe that she allowed, "I hope a train runs over you", to slip out of her mouth so she had to lie to herself in order to believe she never said it. When she told me that I was the reason my mom died, she had tears in her eyes. It was the pain talking. And pain, anger, grief and hurt are not articulate.

Anyway, I found my way to my friend's house, stayed a couple of hours and made my way back home. When I returned late that evening, I got a call from one of the Borg. "Why did you go to New Jersey without permission and why did you come back so late?" I explained that I was seventeen and I didn't see anything wrong with taking the train to visit friends. Then I told aunt Celeste, in front of my grandmother and step-grandfather, "Do you know that she told me that she wishes a train ran over me?" At that my grandmother was up in arms. "Nooooo! I never said that! She's a liar!"

Aunt Celeste on the line then asked me why I was lying on my grandmother. I kept on insisting I wasn't lying. I even asked the step-grandfather, "You were right here. Didn't you hear her say that a train should run over me?" He coyly turned his head away from me. If ever I didn't think I was alone in this world, this was the moment that I did.

After that, I spent a lot of time away from the stresses of the house. I spent a lot of time at Tracy's apartment for peace of mind, even having sleepovers now and again before I officially moved in. Of course my grandmother was livid. She already stamped me as "moved out" although all of my things were still there. Not too long after that, aunt Celeste aka "Ms. I'm going to make you guys rich", decided to move back into my grandmother's house to "help her" deal with Natalie, Nash and I. Now that I am older and able to see these times in hindsight, I realize that my aunt didn't come to the house to be Sally Peacemaker. She came to do quite the opposite.

Celeste is my mother's youngest sister. At this time she was thirty some-odd years old and she was a literal rolling stone. Every time she moved out and tried to make it on her own, she would find her way back to mommy's house. At least she always had a cushion to fall on. Her downfall is that she is a "Keeper Upper of the Jones'". She always lives beyond her means, buying the most expensive clothes, taking the most expensive trips just so she could fit in with the upper crust. She always has to live rich and even if she didn't have a dime, she would still pretend to be rich. Back then I didn't know that she, as well as other family members, only saw my siblings and I as cash cows. So, enter the Dragon...Lady.

Chapter Twenty Three

LET THE GAMES BEGIN

M Y SISTER AND I OCCUPIED the biggest bedroom next to our grandmother's master bedroom. The guest bedroom next to ours was half the size but still overlooked the lush backyard. When aunt Celeste moved in, she approached Natalie who was ten years of age at that time.

"The bedroom next to your room is nice. Would you like to move in there instead?"

My sister quickly answered, "No."

"Are you sure?"

"Yes."

"That bedroom is too big for you especially since Nicole moved out. What are you going to do with all that space?!"

"I don't want to leave this room." My sister said sternly.

After school the next day, my sister came home to find all of her belongings moved to the guest room. It could only hold bunk beds. When I came home a couple days later, my sister blamed me for the reason we got pushed to the smaller room. It was okay because I already blamed myself which was fast becoming a habit of mine. My absence, although it was only for a few days, caused us to lose the big room. I was still very grateful we had a place to rest our heads; even if it was a piece of foam instead of real mattresses.

Celeste offered my sister and I a listening ear. She came like an angel wanting to make 'peace'. She seemed to be there for us in the beginning. When I didn't want to see a child psychologist at the courts anymore because the atmosphere was so cold, she worked it out so we could each see our own individual psychologists in a warmer environment. She took my sister and I clothes shopping now and then, stressing that we are young ladies now and we needed to look the part. She made us think that she was doing this out of her own pocket but as I found out later, she would take the receipts to my grandmother demanding the money back and then some. My grandmother would give her the money from our mutual funds. My aunt actually had free reign to our accounts. Steadily my grandmother would give aunt Celeste more and more allowances and control of Natalie, Nash and I.

When mail would come for me, I would find that it was more difficult than usual to open because the glue was especially sticky. My sister revealed to me that aunt Celeste would boil a pot of water, not for tea but to strategically place my letters over the steam to loosen the glue. She would read my mail and re-glue it before I came home. I don't know how many letters must have been delivered to me but never reached me because aunt Celeste had first dibs. What was her intention? I didn't know at the time. Then my failing college grades would be mailed to the house and before I knew them, my grandmother would yell at me, calling me a failure as soon as I walked through the front door.

"Of course I was failing my grades after my first year in college. I couldn't CONCENTRATE!" And after begging for money from my own mutual funds over and over again and being turned down by my grandmother and aunt, I couldn't buy books. I had to resort to asking classmates to borrow their books for a few minutes to make copies to study for the next class.

I found out that when I hit age 19, my grandmother and aunt were no longer receiving Social Security checks for me anymore so basically, I was no longer welcome in the house. My sister would later see the same dynamic when she was on her way to becoming 19. They would harass her, gossip about her to other relatives and "friends" of the family. One evening when our grandmother was out of town on vacation, our step grandfather locked my sister out of the house and despite her franticly knocking the door and ringing the bell, he refused to get out of his bed to open the door. So my sister, bold and determined as ever, called the police for help. They tried ringing the doorbell too but to no avail. At the first attempt to kick the door down, the step-grandfather appeared as if by a miracle. He received a warning from the officers. Of course he then proceeded to contact our grandmother.

She then contacted all the relatives and my sister was blamed for the embarrassing visit from the authorities.

At 18, Natalie was told to leave. I guess they saw the need to give it a head start with her since she was more of a fighter than I was. My fiery, determined sister refused, informing them that she would move on her own accord when she was good and ready. They kept trying to throw her out and she kept her stance. Aunt Celeste went as far as to sit my sister's boyfriend down while he waited for her to get ready for their date one day and tell him how mentally sick she was. She suggested that he would do well to drop her as a girlfriend before she hurt him or did something crazy to him. She asked him after revealing the false details about my sister,

"Are you sure you want to have *her* as a girlfriend?"

Natalie's boyfriend relayed this sorry attempt by Aunt Celeste to break them up. My sister eventually moved out when she felt financially fit to do so at age 21. My grandmother was not as hard on Nash as my sister and I so he was allowed to stay. When he turned 19, he didn't experience what we did. I am sure the fact that aunt

Celeste moved out by that time had something to do with it.

Anyway, my aunt did lots of things to drive me out of the house. On top of all the other insults, my grandmother started calling me a thief and a liar. I couldn't believe this. It came from left field and it was so not me. I wondered why she added these new names to her bag of tricks. Then one day, my grandmother, "aka" the first world wide web, blurted out, "You think I don't know that you go inside of my file cabinet in my bedroom, taking my money?! Stay out of my bedroom!"

So she thought I was stealing money out of her bedroom. No wonder my step grandfather would follow me when I went upstairs, and periodically peer into my bedroom when I was upstairs alone to see what I was doing. I even tried to put a lock on my bedroom door and my grandmother yelled at me.

"This is my house, not yours! When you get your own house, you can put locks on your own door!"

Of course aunt Celeste had a lock on her bedroom door but I guess that was to keep me out of the "treasures" that were apparently there. My grandmother put two locks on her bedroom door as well.

It turns out that peaceful aunty Celeste was the one breaking into my grandmother's file cabinet, taking money and her personal info, such as her social security number. She slyly told my grandmother that she witnessed me breaking into the cabinet and of course she believed her. What my grandmother didn't know until very recently was that for years, good auntie Celeste used her information to open up credit cards in her name which she shot up to the point of no return. My grandmother's credit, which she meticulously built up throughout her lifetime, is now ruined.

Well, I eventually moved out of the house officially when I was 19 to my aunt's delight. She was victorious - one down, two more to go. I really wanted to stay with my siblings but I couldn't take the harassment anymore. My intention was to continue with school, work hard to finish, go out and make money so I could support myself and my brother and sister.

When I would return home to steadily pick up my belongings, I noticed my little sister becoming more and more hostile towards me. I chalked it up to puberty. She would talk back to me and just seemed angry at me all the time. She even started to belittle me with her sharp tongue. I didn't understand until speaking to my sister recently. After I moved out, my grandmother and aunt Celeste would constantly tell her that I didn't love her or Nash. They made her believe that I left because I wanted to get away from them. How horrible!

These kids lost both their parents in one night less than five years prior and now, here they were, being made to believe that the only person that they looked upon as a mother did not love them. Our cousins would also chime in, convincing my sister that I hated her.

I wondered why every time I came over to the house to take them to the museum or movies my grandmother would tell me to ask my Aunt Celeste for permission. When I would suck it up and ask her for permission (which was ridiculous) I would always get, "No. You're not responsible enough."

I kept on going to my grandmother's house and I kept on getting shot down until I eventually gave up. Natalie and Nash never knew that I would come over with the intention of taking them out for some recreation. This is another fact that only came to life very recently since we had a heart to heart to heart. Communication is very important.

Another issue that was cleared up through communication with my siblings was the drama that surrounded the sale of our old house. When I reached my late twenties, I decided to take on the project of selling the house. My father placed friends there when he was on bail to hold the house until he was released from jail. They were paying the mortgage as rent. I don't think my father realized he would be in prison for so long. Anyway, these people were adamant that the house belonged to them and they refused to leave. This is the reason why no one in my family wanted to take on the burden of trying to sell the property.

The whole process of selling the house took over 2 years because my lawyer had to find a way to get rid of my father's rights to a portion of the sale, as well as getting rid of the people who occupied it.

Eventually, these people decided to cut their losses and one day, they just up and left. But they left the house in a poor state. With their absence, the front yard and back yard quickly became a dumping ground for the neighborhood trash. There were many citations from the Department of Sanitation all over the front porch (so many, a book of pink slips could have been made with them). Squatters began to take up residence. Toothbrushes and beer bottles and some drug paraphernalia were found throughout the house. It was so upsetting to see our home reduced to this.

There were a lot of bumps in the road with the process of sale. Certain members of my family thought that they were owed a piece of the pie from the sale of the house. No one really cared that Natalie, Nash and I had no parents and needed a nest egg to begin our lives. These adults, who already made lives for themselves, were more concerned with bleeding us dry. They were even successful in convincing my sister that I was lying about the process and had, in actuality, already sold the house and taken all the money for myself. She stopped speaking for me for a while and joined in with them as they continued to trash my good name. I can't tell you how many times I was wrongly accused by relatives of being a thief and a liar when these traits were so far removed from me.

Why was my family so preoccupied with keeping Natalie and I separated? Why did they spread these lies about me? How could they claim to love my mother and treat her children like dirt? I'm still trying to answer these questions.

Anyway, I sought out one of my mother's brothers who worked in the construction field for a living to simply fix my mom's roof and paint the walls in the house. He charged us thousands of dollars up front and after the first day told us that we would have to give him a few thousand more before he finished the job. Horrendous! I had to make him believe that he would get the remaining money after he was done in order for him to just finish the job. It was so sad.

The most disappointing aspect of the whole process was not that my relatives demanded money. It was this: aunt Celeste managed to convince my grandmother not to sign the house over to us unless we promised to give her money from the sale. Since she was the Administratrix of my mom's estate as our legal guardian, she could demand this. It didn't matter that Natalie and I were over the age of 19 at this time, she still had this interest in the house legally.

One afternoon, my grandmother asked Natalie and I to join her for a talk in her kitchen. We had no idea what was going on but when we saw aunt Celeste appear, we knew it couldn't be good. I asked, "Why is she here?" My grandmother went on to say,

"Celeste is here because she is my daughter..." She started to get angry at me having the audacity of questioning her presence.

Then my aunt interjected,

"I am here to help my mother explain something to you guys properly."

"She speaks English", I said. "She speaks English pretty well and she's never had a problem explaining herself before." I said sarcastically.

After some arguing, I let them say what they had to say. My grandmother refused to sign off our mother's house to us unless we, with the help of my lawyer, create an addendum stating that we would give her $18,000.00 at the sale of the house. I was livid! But my hands were tied behind my back. I already intended to give my grandmother money from the sale, but dear Aunt

Celeste wanted to make sure that this specific amount was legally bound in writing. I knew that the money would eventually go to my aunt but I couldn't do anything about it. We complied. Natalie, Nash and I signed on the dotted line and finally we were able to finally sell the house to a realty company. I didn't give my construction uncle anymore money and I didn't give anyone else in the family any money either. This widened the rift that was already between me and my mom's family. Aunt Celeste did some really despicable things to us. Too many to number but something that she did when I was still a teenager really hurt me for years to come and to this day, tears still well up when I think about it.

Chapter Twenty Four

FIRE HAZARD

WHEN I WAS ABOUT 19 years of age, Natalie and I were not that close as a result of our family's divisiveness. Beyond this, I can say with confidence that she was always my Number 1 fan when it came to my writings. She read every one of my stories and loved them. She always encouraged me to finish the unfinished ones, develop the ones that were just ideas and publish the ones that were finished. It brought me joy to know that she was so interested in my work. But one day, aunt Celeste created a scheme that she knew would hurt me and divide me from my sister.

At this time I didn't fully move out as yet. Many of my belongings were still at my grandmother's house, including all of my stories and scrap books. I kept them neatly inside of a storage space under the television stand in Natalie's room. When I came over one day to take some more of my stuff, I looked inside of TV stand. Nothing was there. My heart almost leapt out of my body. I ran around the room frantic, searching under the bed, in draws, in the closet; Nothing. When my sister came upstairs I asked her where my writings were. She then told me that aunt Celeste told her that keeping my books in the storage space was a fire hazard. "A fire hazard?!" I yelled. Then my sister took out a few papers that she was able to salvage from my aunt. My sister almost came to tears as well. "I tried to take as much as I could before she threw them in the garbage." I thanked Natalie for saving some of them.

These writings were my life. They were my refuge throughout my tumultuous life. I was inside of each sentence, each word, each sound. 'How could she do this?', I thought. I took the few pages and simply walked outside for hours, crying down the street. I didn't care who saw me. 'How many times can my world be shattered?', I thought.

I confronted aunt Celeste and lo and behold, she told me another story. She said that it was my sister's idea to throw my writings away. My sister, according to her, said that they were a fire hazard. She sounded so sincere. I believed her for a while too. I shouldn't have because for years, I was upset at my sister for lying to me and hurting me this way and for years she was upset at me for not caring about her (as taught by some members of our family).

I am happy to say that now, my sister and I are closer than ever, as sisters should be and my brother makes it an extremely durable threefold chord.

Chapter Twenty Five

REHAB IN A BOTTLE

A FTER 15 YEARS AND MANY trips to the parole board, my father has been deemed rehabilitated and will be given an early release from prison in the summer of 2009. This is the day that I dreaded as a youngster. Fear of him being released would jump me out of my sleep at night. After my mom died, I even started sleep walking and talking. That's how stressed out I was. Even at a time when the body and mind were supposed to rest and unwind, I was highly strung. I am proud to say that I am no longer fearful of him. No one should be feared but God and not even God wants us to have a haunting fear of him. My father, at release, will be sent to a holding facility where he will wait to be deported to his country of birth. This is a little light in a dense fog but what about the people in his country that will be subjected to his behavior. I know that my father has not changed for the better in prison because up to this day, he has not apologized or acknowledged killing my mother. I refused to speak to him all these years but I used to write him, not as a child would a father, but as a psychologist would a patient. I would show him why he should get help and even offer some biblical scriptures that I thought would be helpful to him.

When he noticed the scriptures, I knew that a little half-life light bulb flashed over his head. He saw this as a way to try to manipulate me to get me on his side. So when he wrote back, not only would he complain about my mother's family, listing all the lies they supposedly told on him, he would express how he's learning about God and coming to appreciate him. I saw him coming a mile away. I refused to be susceptible to his manipulating tactics. Suffice it to say, this was a crock. My father did not believe in God. He raised me to be an atheist and for a time I was. On Sunday morning, whenever my mother would get me ready to attend church, my father would insist that I stay home. For the most part he would win. For this reason, my mother started taking me to a Baptist church right before midnight on Saturday nights with one of her good friends, while my father was engaged in his weekend binge drinking- fests in some undisclosed location.

My father was adamant that God did not exist and he bestowed upon me his teachings. He was very dogmatic during his teaching sessions as I was his only pupil. He taught me that I was god and he was god. He said he was also Santa Clause, the Easter Bunny and the Tooth Fairy. This was an eye-opener for a six year old to say the least. My father also admired Hitler and other terrorists so what kind of authority on truth was he? By the age of 10, I came to my senses on my own. My father had and I am sure, still has a lot of hatred in his heart. He manufactures so much hatred that he can not see God in the beauty all around him; such as in the pollen of a flower that bees can not resist, the flickering light in fireflies, the frolicking of the end of summer squirrels and the deep gold hues of the sunset moving across the horizon like slow, thick molasses.

If perchance my father has changed, that's good for him. I really do not want any part of him. I believe in my bones that he hasn't changed at all because, as I

171

said before, he hasn't once acknowledged what he did or apologized. So after paragraphs of blaming everyone but himself for his imprisonment and subsequent erasure from my life and the lives of my siblings, the closest my father would come to acknowledging what he did was, 'I am sorry for what happened to your mother'. Happened? What *happened* to my mother didn't just haphazardly happen by chance. It was executed for almost 2 decades.

Every time my father abused my mom, it was harsher than the abuse before. It was another step closer to her impending murder. And on that wintery Friday night, it came to fruition. I believe that he actually planned my mother's murder that night but who knows for sure? Please, let my mother's example be a warning to everyone reading this who is in an abusive relationship or who knows someone who is. Let's stop this crazy silent epidemic. Now, as my mom's body continues to rot away in her coffin, my father is about to experience the sweet taste of freedom again. Rehab in a bottle.

Chapter Twenty Six

EARLY RELEASE

I RECEIVED OFFICIAL NOTICE FROM THE Parole Board that my father will be released from prison on June 19th 2009. After serving 16 years of his 7 1/4 - 25 year sentence for murdering my mother, he will soon enjoy an early conditional release because of good behavior. Of course my father would be on his best behavior. There was no woman for him to abuse while in prison. I see men who beat women as very, very weak individuals. Inside, they know they are weak but instead of trying to change this, the best way in their minds to make it up is by getting angry and showing their machismo by either finding a weaker woman (if the woman is not completely weak, they pummel her until she is manageable) and punishing her. When a woman cries and begs and pleads for him to stop beating her, raping her etc., this gives the abuser more "power".

The official letter from the Parole Board states that my father will be released to a parole officer. A parole officer? My family and I made sure that my father was put on the immigration deportation list and for years we were told that upon release, he would be automatically placed in a detention center where he would await a plane ride back to his country of birth. So I called the Parole Board who referred me to U.S. Immigration. The immigration officer was quite helpful but when he told me that my father's fate, whether he would be deported or not, rested with an immigration judge, I just shook my head. All these years that my family and I were trekking to parole board hearings every two years, we made sure to have my father's information looked up to make sure he was still on the deportation list. And now there is a possibility that he may remain in the United States?

The immigration representative took my contact information and said he would send me two forms to fill out and return so that I would be updated on my father's status. I await those forms.

For the first time, now that the reality of my father's release is staring me in the face, I am not scared. I have been released from my fear of him and it feels liberating! I just want to forget that he exists. If I see him that would remind me that he does. I want him to live the rest of his life in his little corner of the world knowing that he can never see his children again in the flesh. My siblings and I were robbed of a loving mother. He should be robbed of us.

Chapter Twenty Seven

PAROLE

Okay. Let the countdown begin. In nine days my father will be released from prison after serving only 16 years and 4 months for murdering my mother. The legal system, when it comes to domestic abuse situations, is hideous. He wasn't even legally charged for murder. How sick is that? He was charged with a lesser crime - manslaughter in the first degree.

On the day of the trial, Natalie and I experienced an emotional breakdown, for lack of a better term, as we were being escorted down the hallway to take the stand against our father. I knew that my little sister watched everything that I did and said. Whatever my actions were, Natalie followed suit. I was basically her mother-figure. I tried really hard to be as strong as I could be during that year that my father was out on bail before the trial. I had a lot of pressure on me as the eldest child of three. When my grandmother blamed me for my mother's death because I called her that night instead of the police, as though that would have made a difference, I took the blame punishment and pain like a trooper until the day of the trial.

Our child psychologists prepped us for weeks for this day. All of the prepping in the world could not prepare me to face my father who I had not seen in a year; a father that beat my mother for the last time that night, pulling out her hair and even throwing Natalie up against a wall in our basement as she tried to save our mother; a father whose hands were drenched in my mother's blood, fingerprints on the walls leading from the basement to the first floor; a father whom my intuition told me was contemplating getting rid of me, Natalie and Nash that night as well.

As I stepped out of the room with the psychologists and my sister, walking down the dark grey, speckled hall felt like walking up the steep walls of Mount Everest. The reality of facing my father in a matter of minutes smacked me in the face. I ran back a few feet to the room we left and held on to the door posts with all my strength. I really lost my mind for a moment. No one would force me to go on the stand. My body and my reflexes felt that holding on to a door post would be the best way to protect myself. Natalie followed and held on to me tightly. All the while we were bawling our brains out. I kept screaming, "I don't' want to go! I don't want to go!" over and over again. I couldn't stop myself.

When word reached my father's lawyer, he propositioned him to change his "not guilty" plea to "guilty" so as to save us the trauma of testifying against him. My father did as his lawyer advised. The judge then charged him with manslaughter in the first degree which carried the sentence of 7 1/4 - 25 years. After serving 7 1/4 years, he would be eligible for a paroled release. (Every two years when he was eligible for parole, my family and I testified to the board to have him stay in and we were successful every time. But June 19th is his 'early release date' and because of 'good behavior' he has to be released).

After Natalie and I calmed down, I asked to sit in the back of the court to hear the judge's decree. My father, placed in hand cuffs, was then allowed to speak as long as he wanted before being escorted to prison. Well, no one in that room knew my father as well as I did. Giving my father license to speak was like releasing the floodgates of the heavens in Noah's day. My father was a debater. Most of the time, his views were ludicrous but he would argue them to a pulp. He was a cocky, haughty, know-it-all who always had to have the last say. So here he was on center stage in the courtroom, mad as hell.

He started going on and on and on and on about how he was tricked by his lawyer to plead guilty although he didn't murder my mom. He spoke of his civil rights being abused, etc. etc. The judge actually interjected and equally upset, blasted my father for his arrogance. I remember the judge saying correctly that now he sees that my father is maniacal and calculating and no doubt he planned the murder. He said if he knew of his character before hand, he would have given him the maximum sentence.

Hellooooooooooooooo!!!! His character??? He's a MURDERER! What more do you need to know? Anyway, my father was then thrown out of the courtroom and escorted out with officers, all chained up.

As it stands today, I am happy to say that I have no fear of my father. I actually have no fear of any human being. I refuse to. I don't know my father. I don't know if he has changed. I don't care if he has changed. For all I know, he could have a vendetta against me but I really don't care and I'm really not afraid. This even surprises me and it is such a pleasant surprise. I went through too much in my life to have fear of another human being. He is supposed to be deported to his country of birth at release but as I inquired, this can be overturned by the immigration judge.

My father married an American citizen some years ago while in jail. I'm sure his intention was to use this as a reason why he should be allowed to stay in the United States. I was going to work hard to ensure that he would be deported but I feel liberated to just let the elements take their course in this situation. Whether he stays in the U.S. or not, I really don't care. I just don't think he should ever have the privilege of ever being in the lives of the children that he orphaned by taking our mother away.

Chapter Twenty Eight

THE LETTER IN MY RANDOM
THOUGHT CIRCLE

I SPENT PART OF MY FATHER's Day trying to write a letter to keep my father from being released to a parole officer on U.S. soil. A judge will make the final decision as to whether he should stay here or be deported to his country of birth. I am for deportation. Why should he be allowed to enjoy life in America? Life right now is hard in the U.S. but it is even more difficult in his country of birth so I think he should go back to whence he came. So then, why is it so hard for me to write this letter?

I realize I am putting a lot of pressure on myself to write the most compelling letter ever written in scribal history. I feel that my letter will be that defining thing, being that I am the oldest child. So I must write it in a way that will influence the most unwavering judge. So it has been two days and I have not written anything of substance yet. I stepped back today just to try to figure this out. Yes, I want him to be deported. Yes, I am mad as hell that he is being released from jail for killing my mom-a crime that feels like it happened yesterday. And yes, I hate reliving all of the turmoil I witnessed as a child, living with my parents.

I realize that I am putting off writing this letter because I am afraid it won't be good enough. But hey, I'm not writing a dissertation. But I feel, once again, that all the pressure is on my shoulders to write the best emotionally tugging letter that will influence the immigration judge. I'm writing my thoughts, my experiences and my feelings which hold weight for me so why am I putting so much pressure on myself? Sometimes I just really want to forget that my father ever existed. But then I would have to forget that my mom existed and then I would have to forget about my existence. Do you see the confusion? My mother, my father-they are both a part of me. Regardless of the pain my father has exacted upon me, he has contributed to my existence. He is my only surviving parent and I have not seen him in over 16 years. The child in me yearns for a daddy but the adult in me has to write him off as dead.

Crazy enough, my father did show me love. I was like his little princess. Anything I wanted, he would give me. I didn't ask for much so he would give me more than I ever wanted. He used to drive me around, touring the city, giving me a lesson about the historical significance of each building. He would always send me birthday and Christmas cards in the mail, timing it just right so that it was delivered on the day of or the day before. Every year as a rule, he would have a birthday cake with my favorite pineapple filling, from my favorite bakery waiting for me when I came home from school. He never laid a hand on me to hit me ever but he was like Dr. Jekyll and Mr. Hyde. Although he never hurt me physically, he destroyed me emotionally as he hurt my mother over and over again. So really, is that love?

He really messed up a life that could have been wonderful. The life I'm talking about is not mine but his.

Chapter Twenty Nine

THE DRAGON FLY AT MY WINDOW

FATHER'S DAY USUALLY BRINGS DREAD to Natalie, Nash and I. This year is especially so because my father, as far as I knew, was officially released from prison two days before. So I tried to make the day a special day, to offset the negativity. I invited Natalie, her fiancé and Nash over for dinner but that morning, to my surprise, Natalie showed up unexpectedly. She just wanted to hang out. My daughters and I invited her to go out with us as we shopped for a last minute gift for their dad. My sister's favorite past time is shopping, so it was a go.

I jumped in the shower, turned the water on, and then I heard a loud collective gasp coming from everyone. I didn't really pay it any mind. I thought it was the usual kiddie antics going on. Then my older daughter ran into the bathroom. "Mommy! You have to see this! A dragonfly!"

"A dragonfly? What dragonfly?"

She continued. "There is a dragonfly on the window in the living room. You have to come see it!"

"I just stepped in the shower sweetie. I'll come to see it when I'm done". I said thinking that it would most certainly fly away by the time I was finished. So I took my time and lathered and showered, got dressed and waltzed into the living room. To my surprise, the dragon fly was still there and my sister and the children were going about their regular business, watching TV etc. as if it weren't there.

"Oh my God. Do you see that dragonfly?!" I said stunned and pointing. The dragonfly was resting on the outside of the window netting, its large greenish iridescent, translucent wings outstretched and its long blue body relaxed. It was the biggest dragonfly I have ever seen.

"That's what we were trying to tell you." Natalie and my older daughter said.

"Maybe it's stuck on a web." I said trying to explain why this dragonfly has been perched outside my window for such a long time. About 25 minutes passed and it didn't look as if it was leaving anytime soon. And to top it off, it was such a windy day and my apartment, being on the top floor of the building, usually got the worst of the whipping winds. I thought for sure it was stuck.

"No it's not." Natalie said nonchalantly. "We already checked. It's just looking at us." And it sure did with those big bulging eyes. I walked closer to it, examining it.

"What does a dragonfly symbolize?" I asked. My sister jumped onto my computer in a flash and surfed the web. Apparently in the Western world, it is looked upon as a bad omen.

"Let's go to the East." I said, "They should be more enlightening."

My sister read on. "In China, the dragonfly is looked upon as good luck. They are a sign that water is near and they are also a sign of renewal after a hard tribulation."

"That's it! Oh my God! Renewal after a hard tribulation! That's it!" I said. Natalie agreed.

This was a tremendous moment. Like a break in the invisible barrier between knowing and unknowing. Could this dragonfly have been sent as a sign to let my sister and I know that although our father has been released from prison for murdering our mother, this is now the time for renewal? It seemed so fitting that this dragonfly, arrayed in all its beauty, found rest at my window for my children, Natalie and I to see on the morning of Father's Day. It was too meaningful to be coincidence.

We all did some last minute things before we were ready to leave and like a constant friend, that dragonfly stayed on the window until we left. My father's release initially brought on a deep anger that permeated my being, distracting me at work, at home with my children and it even caused unnecessary tension in my personal life. It gave me headaches, and bodily stress aches that were reminiscent of my tumultuous childhood. But this visit from this striking dragonfly really made me rethink what I was doing to myself. It made me see the need to move on from my chasm of debilitating anger- my hard tribulation to a spring of Renewal. I know that I will probably relapse a little but at least I'm on the right road. Thank you Dragonfly.

Chapter Thirty

PRISON VS. IMMIGRATION DETENTION

I'LL TAKE PRISON FOR $400 Alex. My father decided to stay in jail as opposed to being transferred to a less secure immigration detention center. Why? According to his parole officer, to continue his medical treatment. He knows that if he leaves, he will not be taken care of as he has been for these past 16 years. My father has a few medical problems that need attention such as ulcers and diabetes. He will be re-entering society when it is ailing on so many levels, not to mention Healthcare.

The immigration judge has decided to deny my father's request to stay in the U.S. Whenever his plane ticket is available, he will be flown back to his homeland of Barbados, or so I thought.

My favorite auntie, Abigail, received a call from Immigration Detention upstate New York stating that my father would be released that very morning. Although I signed up with the Victim Services Unit and received a confirmation that I would be informed of my father's prison status and especially when he would be released, I was not. Many things are wrong with the prison system.

Proactively, I would now and then check on my father's status on my own online or I would call his prison because I didn't want to rely on what I already learned to be the flawed prison system. Several months before, when I saw that his earliest release date was fast approaching, I called his prison to make sure that he was going to be deported. They said that wasn't their jurisdiction and forwarded me to U.S. Immigration. I was bounced to at least six different numbers until I finally contacted a living soul. This person assured me that once my father didn't have legal status, he would be sent straight to Immigration Detention where he would await his plane ticket. That's all I wanted- confirmation.

Now, I find out through my aunt that my father was being released from Immigration Detention straight to the streets of New York City? What happened to Barbados? What happened to, "Miss I assure you, there is no way that your father will stay in this country." What happened to, "Even though he married a citizen while in prison, he can not receive legal status as a prisoner."

I was at work when I received the call from my aunt. I was perplexed. My hands started shaking again and my stomach started knotting up. I felt like I was shot back to the past that I've been trying to forget. I had to resign to my supervisor's office behind closed doors and cry my eyes out. I kept trying to get a hold of myself but there are times when we can't control our own bodies.

I left early that day and started working on getting an explanation. Everyone I spoke to in Immigration Detention, at the prison and his new parole officer were all confused. How could this happen? A couple of days passed and someone from Immigration gave me an explanation. My father received legal status in prison when he was allowed to marry a U.S. Citizen. Hmmmmm. Just what I was assured would not happen.

My father knows the ins and outs of the law. He always taught me to learn the law because there are always loopholes. Why are we living in a society where a prisoner, guilty of murder, can outsmart the legal system? In this day and age with 'Homeland Security', why is my father allowed to gain legal status in America when he can't even vote? I'm puzzled.

Anyway, out of initial fear, I had his parole officer put a stipulation in his file, forbidding him from entering Brooklyn or else he would return to prison. Let's see how long this sticks. Now the fear has subsided. Why should I walk down the street watching my back and my front scared of a mere man, robbing my life of happiness and joy. Fear is debilitating and I am tired of people trying to weaken me to my knees. I am confident, I am fearless and more importantly, I am alive. Therefore I will use my example to help others to get out of their abusive relationships. I hope that victims will realize that life is too short to waste living in fear. Life can be cut even shorter if we decide to stay with an abuser.

Chapter Thirty - One

YOU ARE LOVE

AS FAR AS I'M CONCERNED, my father never showed my mother love but she believed that he did love her. I mean, she was a beautiful woman on the outside but more importantly on the inside. She loved to laugh and make people laugh. She was very endearing and people from all walks of life were attracted to her light like moths on a summer night.

I can understand my mother's actions or I should say inactions now that I am an adult and a mother myself. I definitely don't condone her deciding to stay with my father/her murderer, but I understand. I think if you exercise your ability to step into someone else's shoes, you will become a more well-rounded individual because now you understand that your reality is not only all about you but every single soul around you. No man is an island.

Anyway, my mother was easy to love. So why didn't my father love her? It's simple. He didn't love himself. **If your candle is extinguished, how can you light someone else's?** In the same vein, if you don't possess a love for self, how can you give love to others? I believe that God is love and God made us in his image and likeness, so we are made of that most important ingredient – LOVE. Some people may not believe in Jesus Christ, but the fact is that he walked the earth and while on the earth he taught some very valuable lessons. The most important lesson was when he taught that all the commandments could be summarized this way – 'Love God with your whole heart, your whole soul, your whole strength, your whole mind and love your neighbor as yourself.'

I believe this teaching is pertinent to the point I'm trying to make. Love is the answer to all the woes that ail mankind but the love has to start with You. YOU ARE LOVE.

Even if you don't realize it, Love is part of your make up. You exude love from your DNA, through your cells, it runs through your blood, all your organs and permeates through your skin creating a light that surrounds you and attracts people to you. Depending on what we have experienced in life, this light of love may very well be dim or somewhat extinguished. Believe it or not, this is a choice that we make.

Regardless of the hard upbringing we may have had – the abuse we suffered as children or adults, the revolting things that we may have endured and the disgusting names we may have been called, this is not who we are. It's difficult not to let those atrocities erode away how we view ourselves but if we have to fight an uphill battle, we have to fight that uphill battle in order to maintain that Self Love. Sometimes, it's as easy as simply opening your heart to a therapist; talking to a professional person who will keep your confidence. If my mother loved herself, she would not have allowed my father to abuse her. If my father loved himself, he would not have destroyed the one person in the world who truly loved him.

I realize as an adult that I am like my mother in many ways. I am full of genuine love for people. On the flip side, from her example, I learned to avoid relationships with people who do not love themselves. Imagine a scale where on one side, there is a person heavy with love for self and on the other side, someone who is light, without that love. The scales would be lopsided. Ultimately, in my opinion, this relationship (because it lacks balance) will become dysfunctional and fall apart. It's good to take your time and get to know someone before taking that big step of commitment. One red flag, in my opinion, that I always pay attention to is when a man or woman says, "You're too good for me." If they say that, they must be right. More importantly, before we step into the dating scene, we have to make sure that we have a love for ourselves or we'll just be attracting those losers who prey on the insecure and could be potential abusers.

In a world that seems loveless at times, I just felt compelled to talk about the attribute of Love. It surely does exist in all of us. We just have to realize that it is there and encourage it to grow by learning to Love ourselves. In an earlier chapter, *The Empath*, I expressed that I hated my reflection. But as an adult, I have learned to love myself and now I can smile when I look in the mirror. When I look at myself and acknowledge all the pain I have experienced and then look at how far I have come out of that valley of despair, I admire myself. I love myself! You can relearn to love yourself too once you realize that it's official - YOU ARE LOVE!

CLOSING

LTHOUGH I CAN'T REMEMBER WHAT I had for breakfast sometimes, these memories are ones that I can never forget even if I tried. I have experienced a lot more as a child orphaned by domestic violence that I have not mentioned in this book for my sake. I must admit that I have a fantastic long-term memory. Before I didn't know if it was a blessing or a curse but now I am glad for the ability to remember so far back. Many of my memories are painful, but I am thankful for them because I can learn from them.

I have learned that I don't want that type of life for myself as an adult or for my own children. Bad memories are like a detour on a map that can guide you away from ever having to experience them again. They also build character and wisdom in you that you can pass on to others. When you speak, you can lift your head up high and speak with authority. Life can definitely feel like falling down a flight of stairs through thick oatmeal at times, but you will never reach the bottom. God does not allow us to experience more than we can handle.

If you are in an abusive relationship and children are involved, please, if you don't want to think about your welfare, think about your children. Take Heed: Children without loving parents, orphans or Wards of the Court, are open to the world and its many vices and faces and they are not pretty. Get the help through organizations that were not in existence when my mom was alive. Believe me, I miss her more than my words can ever begin to describe.

Made in the USA
Columbia, SC
15 May 2020

97446090R00129